BLUEPRINTS
Music
Key Stage 2
Teacher's Resource
Book

Aelwyn Pugh

Lesley Pugh

Stanley Thornes (Publishers) Ltd

First published in 1995 by:
Stanley Thornes (Publishers) Ltd
Ellenborough House
Wellington Street
CHELTENHAM GL50 1YD
England

A catalogue record for this book is available from the British Library.
ISBN 0–7487–1642–4

Typeset by Tech Set Limited, Gateshead, Tyne & Wear
Printed and bound in Great Britain at The Bath Press, Avon

CONTENTS

To

Rhiannon

INTRODUCTION

WHAT IS BLUEPRINTS: MUSIC? ▶

Blueprints: Music is a practical teachers' resource written to help fulfil the requirements of the National Curriculum in music. It is intended to be used flexibly, either as an ideas bank or as a core resource for a whole scheme for the subject. It is designed particularly for the class teacher who has little confidence in, or experience of, music. At the same time, it can be used by specialists – either directly themselves, or in helping less experienced colleagues build up their confidence in this area. It can also be of help in the production of a whole-school music policy. Because of its structure, *Blueprints: Music* could be used equally well by teachers and schools not following the National Curriculum.

Blueprints: Music consists of materials for Key Stages 1 and 2. For each stage, there is a Teacher's Resource Book, a book of Pupils' Copymasters and an accompanying cassette of songs and music. Again with the needs of the generalist in mind, a glossary of musical terminology and sections on resources have been included.

Blueprints: Music and the National Curriculum

The basic requirements for National Curriculum music at Key Stage 2 are that:

- pupils should be involved in composing, performing, listening and appraising;
- the work should be practically based;
- there should be a close interrelationship between the activities of composing, performing, listening and appraising;
- theoretical work should grow from and feed into such practical activities and be a means to an end rather than an end in itself;
- pupils should be given the opportunity to work individually, in groups and as a whole class;
- they should make appropriate use of information technology to create and record music;
- they should perform and listen to music in a variety of genres and styles, from different periods and cultures;
- the repertoire chosen for performance should be progressively more demanding and chosen in the light of the pupils' needs, backgrounds and stages of musical development.

These general requirements can be put into operation by ensuring that children are given the opportunity to:

- listen carefully to music of various kinds, recognising the main musical elements; distinguishing musical instruments, and responding to changes in character and mood;
- perform from notations, interpreting signs, symbols and simple musical instructions;
- sing and play a range of music, controlling pitch, rhythm and dynamics;
- perform in a group, maintaining a simple part independently of another group;
- understand the principal features of the history of music and appreciate a variety of musical traditions;
- describe, discuss and undertake simple analysis of musical compositions and performances.

How to use this book

The Programme of Study for music in the National Curriculum has been designed to offer general rather than specialised guidelines. This has the advantage of simplicity. On the other hand, a lack of detail does not always make life easier, especially for those teachers who might now be having to teach music for the first time in their careers.

Blueprints: Music aims to give some of this extra guidance. Teachers who simply follow the book through from the front cover to the back can be confident that they are introducing children to a range of concepts and relevant activities which become progressively more complex. However, no book can provide the answer to all problems. Therefore, if you feel that a different sequence or an alternative starting point would be preferable, you should not hesitate to adapt the approach to suit the needs of your specific classes. You should also feel free to extend and supplement the activities. These are provided as a basic resource and should not be viewed as a comprehensive course.

In all, there are 84 Activities in this book, several of which include subsidiary or extension activities. Others are designed not simply as 'once off' activities but as activities to which the teacher and class can return several times in order to extend and reinforce their knowledge, skills and understanding. The pace at which each activity can be presented will also, of course, depend considerably on the experiences of each specific class or group within that class. Therefore there can be no hard and fast rule about the precise point during Key Stage 2 when a specific activity should be presented. However, the following is presented as a rough guide to what might be covered during each year:

Y3: Activities 1–21
Y4: Activities 22–42
Y5: Activities 43–63
Y6: Activities 64–84

Catering for varying experiences, abilities and interests
Within any class, the children are likely to display a wide range of experiences, interests and abilities. *Blueprints: Music* caters for this by presenting a set of core activities. Through the extension work included in each section, these can be developed and adapted to meet the varying needs of individuals.

Key Stage 2 Programme of Study

Pupils' understanding and enjoyment of music should be developed through activities that bring together requirements from both **Performing and Composing** and **Listening and Appraising** wherever possible.

■ **1. Pupils should be given opportunities to:**

  a use sounds and respond to music individually, in pairs, in groups and as a class;
  b make appropriate use of IT to explore and record sounds

■ **2.** When performing, composing, listening and appraising, pupils should be taught to listen with attention to detail, and identify musical ideas, investigating, internalising, *eg hearing in their heads*, and distinguishing the musical elements of:

  a pitch — gradations of pitch, *eg sliding up/down, moving by step/leap; names for pitch such as C, G, doh, soh*;
  b duration — groups of beats, *eg in 2s, 3s, 4s, 5s*; rhythm;
  c dynamics — different levels of volume; accent;
  d tempo — different speeds, *eg lively/calm, slower/faster than*;
  e timbre — different qualities, *eg harsh, mellow, hollow, bright*,
  f texture — different ways sounds are put together, *eg rhythm on rhythm; melody and accompaniment; parts that weave; blocks of sound, chords*;

  and the use of above within

  g structure — different ways sounds are organised in simple forms, *eg question and answer; round; phrase; repetition; ostinato (a musical pattern that is repeated many times); melod*y.

■ **3.** The repertoire chosen for performing and listening should extend pupils' musical experience and knowledge, and develop their appreciation of the richness of our diverse cultural heritage. It should include music in a variety of styles:

  a from different times and cultures, *eg from the European 'classical' tradition; folk and popular music; the countries and regions of the British Isles; cultures across the world*;
  b by well known composers and performers, past and present.

Performing and composing

■ **4.** Pupils should be given opportunities to:

  a control sounds made by the voice and a range of tuned and untuned instruments;

  b perform with others, and develop awareness of audience, venue and occasion;

  c compose in response to a variety of stimuli, and explore a range of resources, *eg voices, instruments, sounds from the environment;*

  d communicate musical ideas to others;

■ **5.** Pupils should be taught to:

  a sing songs, developing control of diction and musical elements, particularly phrasing, *eg giving shape to a song by breathing at the end of a phrase;*

  b play pieces and accompaniments and perform musical patterns by ear and from notations, *eg symbols which define musical elements,* with increasing dexterity and control;

  c sing songs, including songs and rounds in two parts, and play pieces which have several parts, developing the ability to listen to the other performers;

  d rehearse and present their own projects/performances;

  e improvise rhythmic and melodic ideas, *eg add a percussion part to a song;*

  f explore, create, select, combine and organise sounds in musical structures, *eg using repeated sections or verse and chorus;*

  g use sounds and structures to achieve an intended effect, *eg to create a particular atmosphere;*

  h refine and record their compositions using notation(s), where appropriate.

Listening and appraising

  e listen to, and develop understanding of, music from different times and places, applying knowledge to their own work;

  f respond to, and evaluate, live performances and recorded music, including their own and others' compositions and performances.

■ **6.** Pupils should be taught to:

  a identify the sounds made by a variety of instruments individually and in combination, *eg classroom instruments and families of instruments;*

  b identify how musical elements and resources, *eg voices, instruments, performers,* can be used to communicate a mood or effect;

  c recognise ways in which music reflects the time and place in which it is created;

  d compare music from contrasting musical traditions, and respond to differences in character and mood, *eg through dance or other suitable forms of expression;*

  e express ideas and opinions about music, developing a musical vocabulary and the ability to use musical knowledge to support views.

Key Stage 2

■ Attainment Target 1: Performing and Composing

Pupils perform accurately and confidently, making expressive use of the musical elements and showing awareness of phrase. They sing songs and rounds that have two parts, and maintain independent instrumental lines with awareness of the other performers. They select and combine appropriate resources, use musical structures, make expressive use of musical elements and achieve a planned effect. They use symbols when performing and communicating musical ideas.

■ Attainment Target 2: Listening and Appraising

Pupils respond to music, identifying changes in character and mood, and recognise how musical elements and resources are used to communicate moods and ideas. They evaluate their own work, identifying ways in which it can be improved. They begin to recognise how music is affected by time and place, including, where appropriate, the intentions of the composer(s) and performer(s). They listen with attention to detail and describe and compare music from different traditions, using a musical vocabulary.

PROGRAMME OF STUDY GRID

Programme of Study

Pupils' understanding and enjoyment of music should be developed through activities that bring together requirements from both **Performing and Composing** and **Listening and Appraising** wherever possible.

ACTIVITY	a: use sounds and respond to music individually, in pairs, in groups and as a class	b: make appropriate use of IT to record sounds	a: pitch – gradations of pitch, eg sliding up/down, moving by step/leap; names for pitch such as C, G, doh, soh	b: duration – groups of beats, eg in 2s, 3s, 4s, 5s; rhythm	c: dynamics – different levels of volume; accent	d: tempo – different speeds, eg lively/ calm, slower/faster than	e: timbre – different qualities, eg harsh, mellow, hollow, bright	f: different ways sounds are put together, eg rhythm on rhythm; melody and accompaniment; parts that weave; blocks of sound, chords	g: structure – different ways sounds are organised in simple forms, eg question and answer; round; phrase; repetition; ostinato (a musical pattern that is repeated many times); melody	a: from different times and cultures, eg from the European 'classical' tradition; folk and popular music; the countries and regions of the British Isles; cultures across the world	b: by well known composers and performers, past and present
1. Mister Frog's Wedding	•			•				•	•		
2. Blow the Man Down	•			•					•	•	
3. Timbre Game							•				
4. I'm Reaching High, High, High	•		•								
5. Storm at Sea	•	•					•				
6. High, Middle and Low Sounds	•		•								
7. Rhythm Clapping	•			•							
8. How are Sounds Produced?							•				
9. OK You Guys!	•			•	•						
10. Skip to my Lou	•			•	•			•	•	•	
11. Contrasting Timbres	•				•		•		•		
12. Rhythm Devils	•			•							
13. Voice Squares	•				•		•				
14. Maintaining and Transferring the Beat	•			•							
15. Copying and Adding	•			•							
16. Tallis's Canon	•							•	•	•	•
17. Make Up Your Own Canon	•							•	•		
18. Stamping and Clapping Song	•	•			•		•	•			
19. From Very Soft to Very Loud	•				•		•		•		
20. Rhythm Games	•			•				•			
21. How Loud or Soft is it?					•					•	

Programme of Study

Pupils' understanding and enjoyment of music should be developed through activities that bring together requirements from both **Performing and Composing** and **Listening and Appraising** wherever possible.

ACTIVITY / Pupils should be taught to	Pupils should be given opportunities to:		When performing, composing, listening and appraising, pupils should be taught to listen with attention to detail, and identify musical ideas, investigating, internalising, *eg hearing in their heads*, and distinguishing the music elements of							The repertoire chosen for performing and listening should extend pupils' musical experience and knowledge, and develop their appreciation of the richness of our diverse cultural heritage. It should include music in a variety of styles	
	a	b	a	b	c	d	e	f	g	a	b
22. The Windmill	●		●			●			●	●	
23. Instrumental Squares	●						●	●			
24. Joggin' Song	●	●				●					
25. Can You Hear Different Speeds?						●				●	
26. In How Many Ways Can You Make a Sound?	●						●				
27. Changing Speeds	●				●	●		●	●		
28. Wake Up! Wake Up!	●				●				●	●	
29. Bow, Blow, Bang, Pluck, Shake, Scrape	●						●	●		●	
30. Go Tell Aunt Nancy	●			●						●	
31. Celtic Lament			●							●	
32. John Smith Fellow Fine	●			●							
33. Musical Telephones	●						●				
34. Another Way of Writing 'Da' and 'Di-di'	●										
35. Find Your Way Round the Piano			●								
36. The Rain Song			●					●	●		
37. Rain Composition	●				●	●	●	●			
38. Old Molly Hare				●						●	
39. Don't Step on My Musical Toes	●	●		●			●				
40. Leap Down, Jump Down			●			●		●	●		
41. Spring Song								●	●		
42. Listening to Forms in Music									●	●	

xi

Programme of Study

Pupils' understanding and enjoyment of music should be developed through activities that bring together requirements from both **Performing and Composing** and **Listening and Appraising** wherever possible.

ACTIVITY	Pupils should be given opportunities to:		When performing, composing, listening and appraising, pupils should be taught to listen with attention to detail, and identify musical ideas, investigating, internalising, *eg hearing in their heads*, and distinguishing the music elements of							The repertoire chosen for performing and listening should extend pupils' musical experience and knowledge, and develop their appreciation of the richness of our diverse cultural heritage. It should include music in a variety of styles	
	a	b	a	b	c	d	e	f	g	a	b
	use sounds and respond to music individually, in pairs, in groups and as a class	make appropriate use of IT to record sounds	pitch – gradations of pitch, eg sliding up/down, moving by step/leap; names for pitch such as C, G, doh, soh	duration – groups of beats, eg in 2s, 3s, 4s, 5s; rhythm	dynamics – different levels of volume; accent	tempo – different speeds, eg lively/ calm, slower/faster than	timbre – different qualities, eg harsh, mellow, hollow, bright	different ways sounds are put together, eg rhythm on rhythm; melody and accompaniment; parts that weave; blocks of sound, chords	structure – different ways sounds are organised in simple forms, eg question and answer; round; phrase; repetition; ostinato (a musical pattern that is repeated many times); melody	from different times and cultures, eg from the European 'classical' tradition; folk and popular music; the countries and regions of the British Isles; cultures across the world	by well known composers and performers, past and present
43. Improvising Shapes	•							•	•		
44. The Trumpet is Sounding			•		•				•		
45. John Peel						•			•	•	
46. The British Grenadiers		•		•	•			•		•	
47. Improvisation	•					•	•	•	•		
48. Playing the Black Keys on the Piano			•								
49. Come Pack Your Cares Away				•				•	•	•	
50. Plainchant			•	•						•	•
51. Bells and Carillons								•			
52. Chime Composition	•		•								
53. Woodwind Sounds			•				•			•	
54. Reed Instruments			•				•			•	
55. Golden Slumbers			•	•	•	•		•	•	•	
56. London's Burning	•	•	•					•	•	•	
57. Fire Composition	•	•			•	•		•	•	•	•
58. Rigadon by Henry Purcell			•	•				•	•	•	•
59. The Cold Winds Blow				•				•	•	•	
60. Au Claire de la Lune			•					•	•	•	
61. The Seasons	•	•			•	•		•	•	•	•
62. Melodic Composition		•	•					•	•		
63. Bach's Minuet in G								•	•	•	•

Programme of Study

Pupils' understanding and enjoyment of music should be developed through activities that bring together requirements from both **Performing and Composing** and **Listening and Appraising** wherever possible.

ACTIVITY	Pupils should be given opportunities to:		When performing, composing, listening and appraising, pupils should be taught to listen with attention to detail, and identify musical ideas, investigating, internalising, *eg hearing in their heads*, and distinguishing the music elements of							The repertoire chosen for performing and listening should extend pupils' musical experience and knowledge, and develop their appreciation of the richness of our diverse cultural heritage. It should include music in a variety of styles	
Pupils should be taught to	a — use sounds and respond to music individually, in pairs, in groups and as a class	b — make appropriate use of IT to record sounds	a — pitch – gradations of pitch, eg sliding up/down, moving by step/leap; names for pitch such as C, G, doh, soh	b — duration – groups of beats, eg in 2s, 3s, 4s, 5s; rhythm	c — dynamics – different levels of volume; accent	d — tempo – different speeds, eg lively/ calm, slower/faster than	e — timbre – different qualities, eg harsh, mellow, hollow, bright	f — different ways sounds are put together, eg rhythm on rhythm; melody and accompaniment; parts that weave; blocks of sound, chords	g — structure – different ways sounds are organised in simple forms, eg question and answer; round; phrase; repetition; ostinato (a musical pattern that is repeated many times); melody	a — from different times and cultures, eg from the European 'classical' tradition; folk and popular music; the countries and regions of the British Isles; cultures across the world	b — by well known composers and performers, past and present
64. The Harpsichord							●			●	●
65. Fireworks Composition Project	●	●			●	●	●	●	●	●	●
66. The Emperor's Hymn; Haydn	●						●	●		●	●
67. The String Quartet	●						●			●	
68. Variations	●							●	●		
69. The Orchestra	●						●			●	●
70. The Surprise	●				●					●	●
71. Minuet in F	●							●	●	●	●
72. Ode to Joy	●									●	●
73. Schubert Song	●					●		●	●	●	●
74. Robert and Clara Schumann	●		●					●	●	●	●
75. Brahms	●				●	●		●		●	●
76. Sleep Composition	●	●			●	●			●		
77. Major and Minor	●		●						●	●	
78. Is it Major or is it Minor?	●										
79. Composing a Minor Melody	●		●					●	●		
80. Music from India	●							●	●	●	
81. March of the Women	●									●	●
82. Compose a March	●	●		●				●	●		
83. Improvisation on African Scales	●							●	●	●	
84. Go Down Moses	●							●	●	●	

Programme of Study: Performing and composing

Pupils should be given opportunities to:	Control sounds made by the voice and a range of tuned and untuned instruments		Perform with others, and develop awareness of audience, venue and occasion		Compose in response to a variety of stimuli, and explore a range of resources, eg voices, instruments, sounds from the environment		Communicate musical ideas to others	
Pupils should be taught to: / **ACTIVITY**	a — sing songs, developing control of diction and musical elements, particularly phrasing, eg giving shape to a song by breathing at the end of a phrase	b — play pieces and accompaniments and perform musical patterns by ear and from notations, eg symbols which define musical elements, with increasing dexterity and control	c — sing songs, including songs and rounds in two parts, and play pieces which have several parts, developing the ability to listen to other performers	d — rehearse and present their own projects/performances	e — improvise rhythmic and melodic ideas, eg add a percussion part to a song	f — explore, create, select, combine and organise sounds in musical structures, eg using repeated sections or verse and chorus	g — use sounds and structures to achieve an intended effect, eg to create a particular atmosphere	h — refine and record their compositions using notation(s), where appropriate
1. Mister Frog's Wedding	●	●	●					
2. Blow the Man Down	●	●	●					
3. Timbre Game								
4. I'm Reaching High, High, High					●			
5. Storm at Sea				●		●	●	●
6. High, Middle and Low Sounds	●				●			
7. Rhythm Clapping					●			
8. How are Sounds Produced?								
9. OK You Guys!	●							
10. Skip to my Lou	●	●	●		●			
11. Contrasting Timbres		●		●		●	●	●
12. Rhythm Devils		●			●			
13. Voice Squares		●	●	●	●			●
14. Maintaining and Transferring the Beat	●				●			
15. Copying and Adding					●			
16. Tallis's Canon	●	●	●					
17. Make Up Your Own Canon		●	●	●	●	●		●
18. Stamping and Clapping Song	●		●	●	●			●
19. From Very Soft to Very Loud		●		●	●	●		●
20. Rhythm Games		●	●	●	●			●
21. How Loud or Soft is it?								

Programme of Study: Listening and appraising

Pupils should be given opportunities to:	Listen to, and develop understanding of, music from different times and places, applying knowledge to their own work			Respond to, and evaluate, live performances and recorded music, including their own and others' compositions and performances	
Pupils should be taught to: / **ACTIVITY**	**a** identify the sounds made by a variety of instruments individually and in combination, eg classroom instruments and families of instruments	**b** identify how musical elements and resources, eg voices, instruments, performers, can be used to communicate a mood or effect	**c** recognise ways in which music reflects the time and place in which it is created	**d** compare music from contrasting musical traditions, and respond to differences in character and mood, eg through dance or other suitable forms of expression	**e** express ideas and opinions about music, developing a musical vocabulary and the ability to use musical knowledge to support views
1. Mister Frog's Wedding					
2. Blow the Man Down			●		
3. Timbre Game	●				
4. I'm Reaching High, High, High					
5. Storm at Sea		●			●
6. High, Middle and Low Sounds					
7. Rhythm Clapping					
8. How are Sounds Produced?	●				
9. OK You Guys!					
10. Skip to my Lou				●	
11. Contrasting Timbres	●	●			●
12. Rhythm Devils					
13. Voice Squares					●
14. Maintaining and Transferring the Beat					
15. Copying and Adding					
16. Tallis's Canon		●	●		
17. Make Up Your Own Canon					
18. Stamping and Clapping Song		●			●
19. From Very Soft to Very Loud	●				●
20. Rhythm Games					●
21. How Loud or Soft is it?					●

Programme of Study: Performing and composing

Pupils should be given opportunities to: / ACTIVITY	Control sounds made by the voice and a range of tuned and untuned instruments		Perform with others, and develop awareness of audience, venue and occasion		Compose in response to a variety of stimuli, and explore a range of resources, eg voices, instruments, sounds from the environment		Communicate musical ideas to others	
Pupils should be taught to:	a — sing songs, developing control of diction and musical elements, particularly phrasing, eg giving shape to a song by breathing at the end of a phrase	b — play pieces and accompaniments, and perform musical patterns by ear and from notations eg symbols which define musical elements, with increasing dexterity and control	c — sing songs, including songs and rounds in two parts, and play pieces which have several parts, developing the ability to listen to other performers	d — rehearse and present their own projects/performances	e — improvise rhythmic and melodic ideas, eg add a percussion part to a song	f — explore, create, select, combine and organise sounds in musical structures, eg using repeated sections or verse and chorus	g — use sounds and structures to achieve an intended effect, eg to create a particular atmosphere	h — refine and record their compositions using notation(s), where appropriate
22. The Windmill	●	●	●	●				
23. Instrumental Squares		●		●	●			●
24. Joggin' Song	●	●	●				●	
25. Can You Hear Different Speeds?								
26. In How Many Ways Can You Make a Sound?	●							
27. Changing Speeds		●		●	●	●	●	●
28. Wake Up! Wake Up!	●	●	●	●				
29. Bow, Blow, Bang, Pluck, Shake, Scrape	●		●					
30. Go Tell Aunt Nancy	●	●	●					
31. Celtic Lament	●							
32. John Smith Fellow Fine	●	●						
33. Musical Telephones		●						
34. Another Way of Writing 'Da' and 'Di-di'		●			●			
35. Find Your Way Round the Piano		●			●			
36. The Rain Song	●	●	●				●	
37. Rain Composition				●		●	●	●
38. Old Molly Hare	●	●	●					
39. Don't Step on My Musical Toes				●		●		●
40. Leap Down, Jump Down	●	●	●					
41. Spring Song	●	●	●					
42. Listening to Forms in Music								

Programme of Study: Listening and appraising

Pupils should be given opportunities to:	Listen to, and develop understanding of, music from different times and places, applying knowledge to their own work			Respond to, and evaluate, live performances and recorded music, including their own and others' compositions and performances	
Pupils should be taught to: **ACTIVITY**	**a** identify the sounds made by a variety of instruments individually and in combination, *eg classroom instruments and families of instruments*	**b** identify how musical elements and resources, *eg voices, instruments, performers*, can be used to communicate a mood or effect	**c** recognise ways in which music reflects the time and place in which it is created	**d** compare music from contrasting musical traditions, and respond to differences in character and mood, *eg through dance or other suitable forms of expression*	**e** express ideas and opinions about music, developing a musical vocabulary and the ability to use musical knowledge to support views
22. The Windmill					•
23. Instrumental Squares					
24. Joggin' Song		•			•
25. Can You Hear Different Speeds?					•
26. In How Many Ways Can You Make a Sound?	•				
27. Changing Speeds		•			•
28. Wake Up! Wake Up!					
29. Bow, Blow, Bang, Pluck, Shake, Scrape	•				
30. Go Tell Aunt Nancy					
31. Celtic Lament	•	•	•		
32. John Smith Fellow Fine					•
33. Musical Telephones	•				
34. Another Way of Writing 'Da' and 'Di-di'					•
35. Find Your Way Round the Piano					
36. The Rain Song		•			
37. Rain Composition	•	•			•
38. Old Molly Hare					
39. Don't Step on My Musical Toes	•	•			•
40. Leap Down, Jump Down					•
41. Spring Song					•
42. Listening to Forms in Music					•

Programme of Study: Performing and composing

Pupils should be given opportunities to: / ACTIVITY (Pupils should be taught to:)	Control sounds made by the voice and a range of tuned and untuned instruments		Perform with others, and develop awareness of audience, venue and occasion		Compose in response to a variety of stimuli, and explore a range of resources, eg voices, instruments, sounds from the environment		Communicate musical ideas to others	
	a sing songs, developing control of diction and musical elements, particularly phrasing, eg giving shape to a song by breathing at the end of a phrase	**b** play pieces and accompaniments, and perform musical patterns by ear and from notations eg symbols which define musical elements, with increasing dexterity and control	**c** sing songs, including songs and rounds in two parts, and play pieces which have several parts, developing the ability to listen to other performers	**d** rehearse and present their own projects/performances	**e** improvise rhythmic and melodic ideas, eg add a percussion part to a song	**f** explore, create, select, combine and organise sounds in musical structures, eg using repeated sections or verse and chorus	**g** use sounds and structures to achieve an intended effect, eg to create a particular atmosphere	**h** refine and record their compositions using notation(s), where appropriate
43. Improvising Shapes		●		●	●	●		●
44. The Trumpet is Sounding	●	●	●					
45. John Peel	●	●	●					
46. The British Grenadiers	●	●	●	●				
47. Improvisation		●		●		●	●	●
48. Playing the Black Keys on the Piano		●						
49. Come Pack Your Cares Away	●	●	●					
50. Plainchant	●							
51. Bells and Carillons	●	●	●	●				
52. Chime Composition				●	●	●	●	●
53. Woodwind Sounds								
54. Reed Instruments								
55. Golden Slumbers	●	●	●					
56. London's Burning	●	●	●	●		●		●
57. Fire Composition				●		●	●	●
58. Rigadon by Henry Purcell	●	●	●	●				
59. The Cold Winds Blow	●	●	●					
60. Au Claire de la Lune	●	●						
61. The Seasons				●	●	●	●	●
62. Melodic Composition				●	●	●		●
63. Bach's Minuet in G								

Programme of Study: Listening and appraising

Pupils should be given opportunities to:	Listen to, and develop understanding of, music from different times and places, applying knowledge to their own work			Respond to, and evaluate, live performances and recorded music, including their own and others' compositions and performances	
Pupils should be taught to: **ACTIVITY**	a identify the sounds made by a variety of instruments individually and in combination, eg classroom instruments and families of instruments	b identify how musical elements and resources, eg voices, instruments, performers, can be used to communicate a mood or effect	c recognise ways in which music reflects the time and place in which it is created	d compare music from contrasting musical traditions, and respond to differences in character and mood, eg through dance or other suitable forms of expression	e express ideas and opinions about music, developing a musical vocabulary and the ability to use musical knowledge to support views
43. Improvising Shapes	●				●
44. The Trumpet is Sounding					
45. John Peel	●				
46. The British Grenadiers		●			●
47. Improvisation	●	●			●
48. Playing the Black Keys on the Piano					
49. Come Pack Your Cares Away				●	●
50. Plainchant		●	●	●	●
51. Bells and Carillons					●
52. Chime Composition	●				●
53. Woodwind Sounds	●		●	●	
54. Reed Instruments	●				●
55. Golden Slumbers	●	●			
56. London's Burning					●
57. Fire Composition	●	●	●		●
58. Rigadon by Henry Purcell	●	●	●		●
59. The Cold Winds Blow					
60. Au Claire de la Lune				●	●
61. The Seasons	●	●	●		●
62. Melodic Composition					
63. Bach's Minuet in G	●	●	●		

Programme of Study: Performing and composing

Pupils should be given opportunities to:	Control sounds made by the voice and a range of tuned and untuned instruments		Perform with others, and develop awareness of audience, venue and occasion		Compose in response to a variety of stimuli, and explore a range of resources, eg voices, instruments, sounds from the environment		Communicate musical ideas to others	
Pupils should be taught to: → ACTIVITY	a — sing songs from memory, developing control of breathing, dynamics, rhythm and pitch	b — play pieces and accompaniments, and perform musical patterns by ear and from notations eg symbols which define musical elements, with increasing dexterity and control	c — sing songs, including songs and rounds in two parts, and play pieces which have several parts, developing the ability to listen to other performers	d — rehearse and present their own projects/performances	e — improvise rhythmic and melodic ideas, eg add a percussion part to a song	f — explore, create, select, combine and organise sounds in musical structures, eg using repeated sections or verse and chorus	g — use sounds and structures to achieve an intended effect, eg to create a particular atmosphere	h — refine and record their compositions using notation(s), where appropriate
64. The Harpsichord								
65. Fireworks Composition Project				●		●	●	●
66. The Emperor's Hymn; Haydn	●	●	●					
67. The String Quartet								
68. Variations								
69. The Orchestra								
70. The Surprise								
71. Minuet in F		●		●				
72. Ode to Joy	●						●	
73. Schubert Song	●	●	●	●				
74. Robert and Clara Schumann		●		●				
75. Brahms	●	●	●	●				
76. Sleep Composition				●		●	●	●
77. Major and Minor	●	●	●	●	●			
78. Is it Major or is it Minor?								
79. Composing a Minor Melody				●	●	●	●	●
80. Music from India								
81. March of the Women	●							
82. Compose a March				●	●	●	●	●
83. Improvisation on African Scales				●	●	●		●
84. Go Down Moses	●	●	●					

Programme of Study: Listening and appraising

Pupils should be given opportunities to:	Listen to, and develop understanding of, music from different times and places, applying knowledge to their own work			Respond to, and evaluate, live performances and recorded music, including their own and others' compositions and performances	
Pupils should be taught to: ACTIVITY	a identify the sounds made by a variety of instruments individually and in combination, eg classroom instruments and families of instruments	b identify how musical elements and resources, eg voices, instruments, performers, can be used to communicate a mood or effect	c recognise ways in which music reflects the time and place in which it is created	d compare music from contrasting musical traditions, and respond to differences in character and mood, eg through dance or other suitable forms of expression	e express ideas and opinions about music, developing a musical vocabulary and the ability to use musical knowledge to support views
64. The Harpsichord	●		●		●
65. Fireworks Composition Project	●	●		●	●
66. The Emperor's Hymn; Haydn	●		●		
67. The String Quartet	●	●			●
68. Variations		●			●
69. The Orchestra	●			●	
70. The Surprise	●	●	●	●	
71. Minuet in F				●	●
72. Ode to Joy		●	●	●	
73. Schubert Song		●	●		●
74. Robert and Clara Schumann		●		●	●
75. Brahms	●	●	●		●
76. Sleep Composition		●			●
77. Major and Minor		●			
78. Is it Major or is it Minor?		●		●	●
79. Composing a Minor Melody					●
80. Music from India	●		●	●	
81. March of the Women		●	●	●	●
82. Compose a March					●
83. Improvisation on African Scales			●	●	●
84. Go Down Moses		●	●	●	●

PERFORMING, LISTENING AND COMPOSING

The three main foci for music teaching are: performing (vocal and instrumental), listening and composing. The next section offers advice on how these three types of activity might be approached in the classroom and what types of resources you will need to help you.

THE TEACHING OF SINGING

Why should we teach singing?
Since it is actually part of us, the voice is the most intimately controllable of instruments and allows for musical involvement of the most personal kind. Because of this, singing is likely to have a profound effect on our musical development. Singing allows us to extend the use of the voice, making it into an expressive instrument. This is likely to have a beneficial effect on our use of the voice in everyday situations and not just in a musical context. Lastly, the voice is the most easily portable and cheapest of instruments.

The National Curriculum and singing
In the last twenty years, there has been evidence of a decline in singing in the classroom. 'Serious' music making has often been equated with instrumental performance, with vocal work being relegated to second place. In fact, the two aspects of music are complementary to each other and should not be regarded as alternative options. This is clearly emphasised in National Curriculum documentation.

When should we teach singing?
Singing should be a central activity in the programme of music lessons you offer your children and, further on, you will find advice on how and when to present songs during a lesson. Many schools, of course, also include singing as part of their extra-curricular activities and even more include it as part of a formalised 'hymn practice'.

The great advantages of participating in an extra-curricular choir are that the children are given further opportunities to extend their skills, to encounter a wider range of music, to work with others of varying ages and thereby to enrich both their musical and social experiences. In the case of 'hymn practices', children could gain similar advantages. However, the extent to which this is likely to happen depends very heavily on how the activity is approached. Involving whole year groups or a whole key stage in singing together can have social advantages of reaffirming group identity. In the right context, it might also contribute to the children's spiritual growth. But the extent to which it contributes to their musical development is questionable. There are few, if any, other areas of the curriculum where we would be happy to involve large numbers of

Unless you are prepared to sing, your pupils will never have a go.

children of a wide range of ages and abilities in pursuing an undifferentiated activity, with only one or two teachers present. We would certainly be sceptical about the extent to which such an arrangement could make a genuine contribution to the development of children's knowledge, skills and understanding. We would never contemplate it as an approach to the teaching of maths or English. Therefore why should we do so for music? Poor teaching is poor teaching whatever the subject to which it is applied.

This is not to say that there can be no value whatsoever in hymn practices or combined group singing. It can considerably enrich the children's experiences if they have had a considerable amount of small group or individual attention beforehand. Even then, it is important that there is regular reinforcement of the points about phrasing, breathing, volume etc., which are addressed later in this section. In short, hymn practices, if they are used, should be a celebration and reinforcement of what has been learnt in the classroom and should not be treated as an alternative to class or small group singing activities.

1

How can I teach singing if I haven't got a voice?
It is surprising how many teachers seem to think that, unless they have a voice like Pavarotti or Kiri Te Kanawa, they have no right to describe themselves as singers and therefore never perform to their pupils. Few of us would ever expect to be invited to read 'Book at Bedtime' on the radio but we happily read stories to our classes. In the same way, we do not mind admitting to playing football or cricket although we would never make a Ryan Giggs or Mike Atherton. So why should singing be any different?

Singing is a practical activity. The only way to learn how to do it is to make practical experiments. Use your voice as often as possible. Do not be put off by other people's comments and draw comfort from the tremendous support that young children give their teachers.

How can I teach singing when I can't play the piano?
Answer: you don't have to use it!

Too often, teachers over-estimate the importance and usefulness of the piano in music lessons. In fact this instrument has many disadvantages. A note on the piano, once struck, quickly dies away. This constant falling off of the sound is quite different from the effect which we should be striving for in singing. Therefore, a melody played on the piano is not a particularly good example for pupils to imitate.

The volume of sound produced by the piano often makes it difficult for the teacher to gain an accurate notion of how the class is performing. It is all too easy to convince oneself that the louder one plays, the louder the class is singing. This is rarely the case. Confident in the knowledge that the teacher is deafened by her own playing, many children quickly become very competent mime artists.

There is a great danger of becoming anchored behind a piano and creating a 'no-man's land' between the teacher and the pupils.

Unless a teacher is confident and knows a piece extremely well, there is a danger that the position of the fingers on the keyboard becomes of totally absorbing interest, at the expense of eye contact and a close rapport with the class.

Points to bear in mind if you do use the piano
Position the piano so that you can see and maintain contact with the class. Some teachers like to face their classes and to stand behind the piano while playing. Others prefer to place the piano at an oblique angle and to play in a sitting position. Try both approaches and decide which suits you best. Whichever approach you take, do not stay anchored to the instrument. Move around your class so that you can hear the children and they can hear you. Make sure that you can play the music accurately without having to fumble for the notes. Practise playing songs in a variety of keys so that

you can adapt to voices of varying ranges, and try to balance accompanied work with unaccompanied singing.

Advantages of the guitar in the classroom
This instrument has the advantage of enabling you to be near your pupils and to maintain close contact with them when performing. Since it is an ideal accompanying instrument, there is little danger of its overpowering your own voice when singing.

Because it is so portable, there is no reason for you to stay in one spot. When helping small groups or individuals in various parts of the room, you can take the instrument up to them and give any required support, without necessarily drawing the attention of the rest of the class. Through the use of the capo, you can transpose a tune into keys which suit the children's voices.

If you do not play the piano or guitar, sing unaccompanied
Unaccompanied singing should be the basis and central focus of all singing lessons, even when the teacher is an accomplished instrumentalist. Working without accompaniment helps develop accuracy of pitch and a high degree of listening – both essential for any musician.

A policy of 'Do as I say and not as I do' will never succeed where singing is concerned.

TEACHING A SONG

Reasons for teaching a song

There are several possible reasons for teaching a song to a class:

- to develop vocal skills
- to help children learn how to read music notation
- to extend the children's knowledge of their culture
- to enable them to have an enjoyable experience.

Whatever your reasons, be clear in your mind what you are trying to achieve, since this will influence both the type of song that you teach and how you set about presenting it to your class.

Teaching a song by rote

Much of your singing teaching will have to be done by rote. Below is one possible approach to this: it is not meant to be followed slavishly but it can be a useful starting point and has been well tried by a wide range of teachers – particularly teachers who regard themselves as 'non-specialists'.

Stage I: Introduce the song by means of a picture, a story or related event or activity. Presenting a song 'out of the blue' can be very confusing for children. Therefore this is an essential stage. On the other hand, do not let the preamble cause an unnecessary delay in the presentation of the song.

Stage II: Sing the entire song to the children. In doing so, try to make it as interesting as possible. If the song tells a story then make sure that you involve the children in it, just as you would if you were speaking it. Use interesting facial expressions and gestures if necessary. Always make sure that you are looking at them and communicating with them. In doing this, you will be bringing your existing skills to bear on a less familiar area and helping to build your own confidence.

Stage III: Lead a brief discussion of the words, drawing attention to any particular aspect of the text that you might want to emphasise, e.g. contrasts of volume in a song about echoes.

Stage IV: Sing the song to the class again. As with other areas of the curriculum, children – especially young children – need and enjoy repetition.

Stage V: (a) Sing the first line of the song – more than once if necessary. From the outset get the children used to preparing for their performance by beating several introductory beats and counting regularly 1–2 or 1–2–3 or 1–2–3–4 at the speed at which the rhyme/song is to be performed. You will probably find that the children will eventually count in with you. This should not be discouraged. At a later stage, ask them to 'think' introductory beats or mark them silently with movements. The appropriate count is indicated for each song in the book, as is the chime bar which you can use to give yourself and the children the appropriate starting note.

(b) Sing the first note and count the class in on that note. The children now sing the first line. Again, do this several times if necessary.

Stage VI: Sing the second line a few times and ask the children to sing it back to you – several times if necessary. Do not forget that, at each stage, you will need to give the first note and count the class in.

Stage VII: The first two lines are now combined – first by you and then by the children.

Stage VIII: Gradually, through a series of teacher demonstrations and pupil imitations, the lines are built up into the whole song. You could use a variety of sequences for this. For example a three line verse might be presented in this order: Line A, Line B, Line C, Lines B and C, Lines A to C. A six line song might be presented like this: A, B, AB, CD, ABCD, EF, EF, whole verse. When you have gained more confidence, experiment with other sequences.

Don't forget to disguise the repetition

By presenting a song in the ways described, you are making it more manageable for the children and easier for them to grasp. With so much emphasis on repetition, however, it would be very easy for the lesson to become monotonous, so do not forget to disguise the repetitions, e.g.:

- Vary the volume of the repetitions – sometimes sing them loudly; at others times sing them softly.
- Where appropriate, let the music get louder or softer.
- Ask groups of children to sing, rather than the whole class.
- Invite individuals to sing. This is far easier than teachers often imagine. A child who is complimented for his/her singing in the group will be more than ready to take up the invitation to sing alone. Praising that child and then inviting others to sing a solo usually leads to too many rather than too few volunteers.
- Ask the children who come to school by bus to sing together.
- Ask those with birthdays in a specific month or group of months to sing together.
- Ask all the children on the blue table, the orange table, the red table etc. to sing together.
- Intersperse the repetitions with short anecdotes or jokes.
- Dispense with the words occasionally and ask the children to hum or sing to one syllable such as 'coo'.

This list is by no means exhaustive but should serve to illustrate the point that essential repetition need not necessarily be boring.

Two further requirements

First, be supportive of the children when they sing. Do not be content with a standard of work which can be improved. For the time being, accept the work so long as they have done their best, but then strive to improve it. This is a delicate balancing exercise which is as important in music as in any other area of the curriculum.

Second, maintain a lively pace in the lesson. Music making is a physical activity and should be as lively and exciting as a well-run games lesson.

Introducing a new song
Learning uses up children's energies, so it is best to introduce a new song at the beginning of a lesson. With longer songs, do not try to teach them in their entirety in one lesson. Pushing children beyond their span of attention is counterproductive and breaks between learning can actually speed up the overall process.

IMPROVING CHILDREN'S PERFORMANCE ▶

When children have performed a song or a section of it, do not be too hasty in pointing out faults. Instead, praise them, wherever possible, for their 'feel' for the song and for their surmounting of various difficulties in singing it. Only then should you begin to suggest how their singing could be improved. Below is a set of possible strategies which you might wish to use in improving certain aspects of the children's performance. It is not advisable to make more than two or three of these 'corrections' at a time and in no way can all the approaches to a particular problem be implemented in one lesson. Therefore, look on these as a set of approaches which you could draw upon or adapt to suit your particular circumstances.

Improving the volume of the singing
When children are not used to singing – or when it is approached half-heartedly – they tend to produce a very quiet sound. Even classes which sing regularly will lapse from time to time. Without at least a moderately loud sound, the children will never gain much confidence and it will be difficult to try to remedy other problems, such as unclear diction or inappropriate phrasing. One possible way to improve the volume of singing is this:

1. Take a line of the song.
2. Divide your class into groups of 4 or 5 children.
3. Sing the line to the children a few times and ask the first group to sing it back to you.
4. Repeat the process with the next group.
5. Ask both groups to sing together after you have again demonstrated to them.
6. Continue the process around the class via:
   (a) teacher demonstration
   (b) demonstration by a specific group
   (c) performance by all groups who have performed up to that point.

Be very encouraging with each group and compliment them on their work; unless of course they are deliberately making little effort. Remember that the object of the above exercise is to produce a confident volume of sound, not to get the class to the point where all the children are shouting in competition with each other.

Improving children's stance when singing
'Hold your heads up' is an exhortation often heard during singing activities, but it is not a particularly useful one. If the head is held too high, the throat becomes constricted and leads to the production of a very 'contorted' sound. Any 'high' notes will also seem particularly difficult to children with their heads at this angle since they will have the impression of all the notes soaring way out of reach above them.

The children will produce a better sound and find it easier to sing high notes if they incline their heads slightly forwards and look towards a point on the floor about 6–10 feet ahead of them. (A strategically placed object can work wonders in keeping a child's attention on one spot.)

Singing relies on effective breathing. This cannot be achieved when the diaphragm is contorted as, for example, when a child is slouching over a desk or sitting slumped in a chair. If you tried to run with your body bent double, you would soon run out of breath. The same holds true if you try to sing in such a position. Therefore do not be afraid to ask your children to stand when singing. We expect children to stand in PE and games lessons so there is no reason why we should not do the same in a music session. Of course, it is important to vary the activities, so that the children are not standing too long or unnecessarily. As in any other aspect of your work, ring the changes and make sure that there is plenty of variety.

Occasionally you might ask the children to sit with their backs straight. Unfortunately they will tend to forget, with the result that either the notion of a good posture is gradually abandoned or you have to keep nagging at them, to the boredom and frustration of all concerned. Standing achieves the desired end with far less fuss.

Improving diction
If the words of a song are to be audible to a listener, the consonants in them need to be emphasised. There are several simple strategies which will help children do this.

1. Ask the children to lip-read silent messages sent by yourself. Then arrange for pairs of children to communicate with each other in this way. This will encourage them to exaggerate their mouth gestures.
2. Maintaining these exaggerated mouth gestures, the children now whisper a message/line of a song pronouncing the consonants only. The vowels should not produce any sound at all. To ensure this, ask the children to place their hands on their throats. If there is any vibration while the vowels are being mouthed, the children will need to correct themselves.

4

3. These activities can again be made into a game, e.g.
   (a) by sending messages around the class in 'consonant whispers';
   (b) by asking a child to listen behind a screen or outside a door to hear whether a message whispered by the class can be understood.

Remember that these games and exercises are a means to an end and not ends in themselves. Therefore, at each stage, make sure that the techniques being developed are applied to sung as well as spoken activities.

Quite often when children come to applying the techniques to singing, they will over-exaggerate them. Do not let this worry you. The exaggeration can be toned down by you, or the children will do it for themselves.

Improving phrasing

Too often the performance of a song is spoiled by insufficient attention to phrasing. Thus, for example, a class will sing: 'The fox went out (breath) one chilly night' instead of 'The fox went out one chilly night' (breath).

A singer should try, as far as possible, to breathe at the natural breaks in sentences and not cut across the punctuation of a line. Where two lines follow on from one another, the link should be maintained, e.g. you should sing: 'Good King Wenceslas looked out on the feast of Stephen', not 'Good King Wenceslas looked out (breath) on the feast of Stephen'. Careful attention to

these simple points can improve the quality of a performance considerably.

One of the main reasons for unnecessary and inappropriate breaks in a line is that children run out of breath. To combat this, try to help them breathe more efficiently.

Improving breathing

Many tomes have been devoted to this subject. The most important points to remember are these:

1. When breathing in, fill the lower part of the lungs first, then the upper part. This is helped by placing a hand on the tummy just below the ribcage and pushing this out with breath before pushing out the upper part of the chest. This should be done without raising the shoulders.
2. When breathing out, the process is reversed, with the upper lungs being emptied first.
3. When breathing out, children often do so too quickly. One way to help overcome this is to let the children breathe onto a mirror and keep it misted up as they exhale slowly and gently.

With increasing experience and confidence, you will no doubt discover further techniques to help improve your children's work. Once again, remember that the approaches described above should not all be used at once and do not try to tackle too many problems in one go. But, whenever you are singing, be alert to ways in which the work might be developed in future lessons.

WORKING WITH INSTRUMENTS ▶

As has already been seen, the National Curriculum Programme of Study places considerable emphasis on giving children the opportunity to work with tuned (pitched) and untuned (unpitched) instruments. This section will try to give the inexperienced musician some guidance on the types of instruments which fall into these categories and how they might be approached. Further help on using instruments is contained within the individual activities.

From the time they enter school, children should have access to a wide range of instruments which are well made; are attractive to hold, look at, listen to and play; and are of an appropriate size for small hands. These instruments need to be readily accessible, so that children can experiment with them and get to know them well.

Inevitably instruments make a noise. But there is a difference between controlled noise and chaos. In a PE, games or dance lesson, children are taught when to start, stop, put the equipment down, experiment with ideas, observe each other and observe the teacher. The same approaches are equally applicable to working with instruments and to several other aspects of music making.

As with any other equipment, musical instruments need to be handled with care. But this can sometimes be

taken to extremes. A child who is only ever allowed free access to an old, unattractive instrument while the 'best' ones are confined to 'the music lesson' can be forgiven for losing interest.

Again, like any other equipment, instruments do wear out. Therefore, every school should have a policy of investment and replacement for musical instruments.

What types of instrument should you use?

A basic stock of classroom instruments should contain a variety of wooden and metal, untuned (unpitched) and tuned (pitched) instruments. It is better to invest in one or two examples of several types of instruments than in trying to give every child an example of one specific instrument.

Below is a list of the types of instruments useful at Key Stage 2, together with brief details of how they might be played. But do not confine yourself or your pupils to one way of performing. Composers are always looking for ways of extending the range of sounds available to them. This process of investigation should begin at the school level and should not be arrested by an over-concern with confining children to one 'conventional' way of playing a particular instrument.

UNTUNED (UNPITCHED) PERCUSSION

Afuchie (or cabasa)
This can be played by shaking it. Alternatively, and more usually, it is played by rotating the beads against the central metal cylinder to produce a grating sound.

Hand-held castanets can be played in a variety of ways, e.g. by holding the handle in one hand and flicking it forward so that the two clappers click against the central handle. Or they could be held in one hand and struck against the thigh or the palm of the other hand.

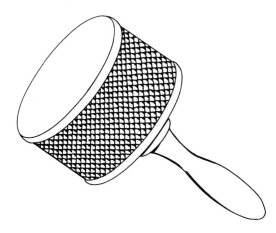

Cabasa (or shekere)
This is made of a dried gourd shell, strung with a loose mesh of seeds or beads. It is played by being shaken.

Claves (rhythm sticks)
These are played by striking one against the other.

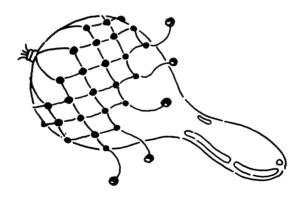

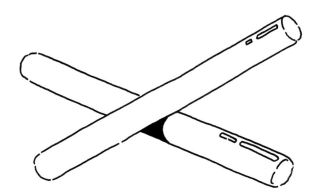

Castanets
Castanets are played by holding them between the thumb and the first three fingers and closing them together to create a clicking sound. The easiest type for children to handle are those which have a tight elasticated joint at the base. Other types, held together by string, can be difficult for some children to manage.

Cymbals
These can be played by clashing them together or by holding one of them by the handle, so that it is parallel to the floor, and striking it with a beater.

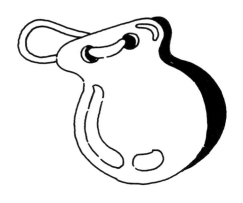

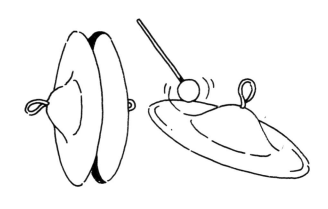

It is also possible to have finger cymbals. These come in pairs and are attached to finger and thumb and struck together.

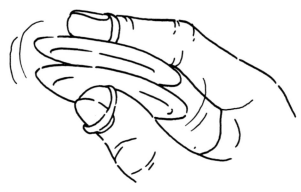

Finger cymbals

Indian bells consist of a pair of small cymbals suspended at both ends of the same piece of string. They are played by striking one against the other.

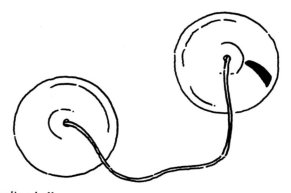

Indian bells

Drums

There is a wide variety of drums available. Children should be given access to several types and sizes, e.g. bongo drums and hand drums. They are played by being tapped with the hand or struck with a beater.

Guiro (resi-resi scraper or rasp)

This consists of a tube with a serrated edge, along which is drawn a scraper to produce a rasping sound. Guiros come in several sizes and shapes, including cylindrical and fish shapes. Guiros are made of a variety of materials, including metal and wood. Metal guiros often have more than one type of serrated surface, so that it is possible to produce a greater variety of sounds on them.

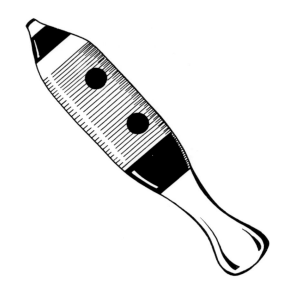

Jingle bells

These come in many forms – with or without handles. They are played by being shaken.

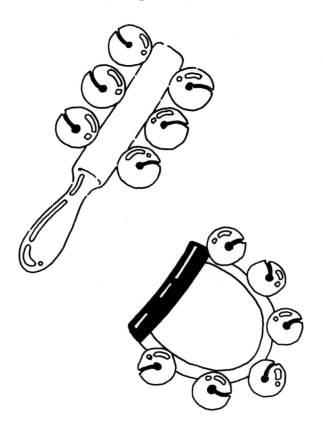

7

Maracas

Maracas are a type of rattle. Originally made from gourds, they now come in a variety of materials, including plastic and wood. They are usually sold in pairs. Ideally they should be played by holding one in each hand and shaking them alternately. One maraca can be played singly by holding it in one hand and tapping it against the palm of the other hand.

Rattles

These come in many forms and are made from a variety of materials – plastic, wood and cane.

Shakers

A common and durable shaker useful in the classroom is one made of a light-weight metal tube.

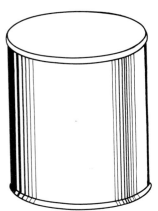

Tambour

A tambour is a shallow drum. It looks rather like a tambourine without its jingles. Like a drum, it can be played with the hands or with beaters.

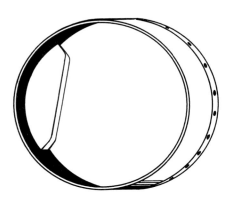

Tambourine

These come in several varieties – with a skin, without a skin and in interesting shapes like the half-moon tambourine.

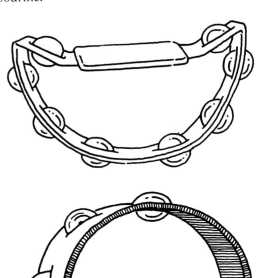

TUNED (PITCHED) INSTRUMENTS

Agogo

An agogo consists of two hollow tubes of different sizes mounted on a handle. The two tubes are struck with a beater to produce two notes: a higher and a lower pitched one. The tubes on wooden agogos often have serrated sides so that they can double as guiros (see above).

Agogo

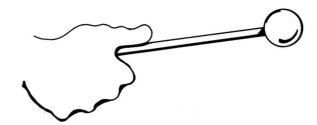

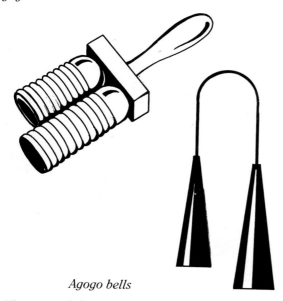

Agogo bells

There are also metal versions known as agogo bells or metal agogos. In some instances, metal agogos can have more than two bells.

Beaters

Tuned percussion instruments are usually played with beaters. These will vary in terms of the size of the head, the length of the stick and the hardness of the material from which the head is made. Xylophones, glockenspiels and metallophones usually come with a pair of beaters suitable for use with those specific instruments. You can, however, produce a wide range of effects from one instrument by varying the type of beater used. Generally speaking, the harder the beater head, the more piercing the sound produced on the instrument.

It is advisable to buy extra sets of beaters to cover losses and to give children a wider range of possibilities for experimenting. To minimise loss or breakages, and to avoid unnecessary expenditure, make sure that you have a clear system for distributing and collecting beaters when using them in the classroom.

A single beater would be appropriate for use with a single chime bar and also on occasion with glockenspiels, xylophones and metallophones. But, as the children become more adept at manipulating the sticks, encourage them to use a pair of beaters at a time. This allows for the playing of more than one note simultaneously (a chord) and makes faster music easier to play.

At an even later stage in their development, children could be encouraged to hold more than one beater in one hand.

Encourage the children to hold the beaters as shown in the above illustration and to make the beater bounce on the bar of the instrument so that it produces a clear note. This is not to say that the children should not also be given the chance to experiment with other ways of making a sound. If, for example, a child wants to produce a very short note when making up music on a glockenspiel, he or she might prefer to strike the bar and keep the beater on it rather than letting it bounce. There are further ways of experimenting with these and other instruments which will be suggested elsewhere in the book.

Cow bells

Unlike alpine cow bells, percussion cow bells do not have clappers. Instead the sound is produced by striking them on the outer surface with a beater. Different sized cow bells produce different pitched sounds. The larger the cow bell, the lower the sound.

Individual cow bells can be held in the hand or they can be mounted on a particular type of stand specially produced for the purpose.

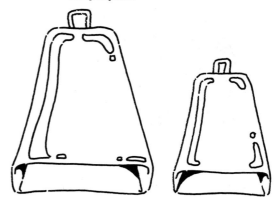

Temple blocks

These are hollow wooden instruments which sound when struck on the outer surface. Like cowbells, they come in different sizes and can be mounted on a stand.

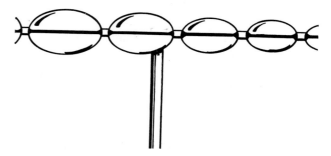

Chime bar

A chime bar consists of a hollow box or tube to which is attached a metal bar tuned to a particular pitch. The pitch of the note is usually stamped on the surface of the bar (C, D, E, etc.). It is possible to have chime bars covering a wide range of pitches. Each note is a separate instrument, although several can be grouped together to make scales of notes. A chime bar is usually played by being struck with a beater. The sound will keep vibrating for a considerable time after being struck. It can, however, be made shorter by putting a finger on the surface as soon as it has been struck.

the player looks at the instrument. The bars then become progressively smaller, and progressively higher in pitch, as their position moves to the right of the instrument. The smallest bar – and therefore the highest pitched note – is the one at the far right of the instrument.

A *diatonic* glockenspiel is one which has the notes CDEFGABCDEFGA, i.e. notes which correspond in pitch to the white notes on a piano.

A *chromatic* glockenspiel has the above notes plus a second row of notes which correspond in pitch to the black notes on the piano.

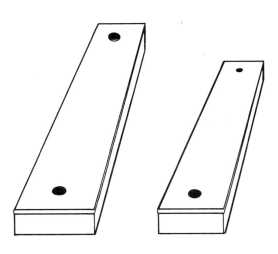

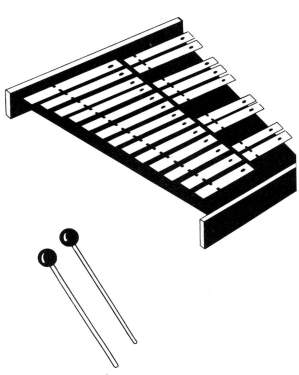

An alto chromatic glockenspiel

Glockenspiel

A glockenspiel consists of a long open box divided into resonance chambers. Balanced across the upper edges of the box are nickel-plated steel bars of varying sizes. These are sounded by being struck with beaters. As with chime bars, the larger the bar on a glockenspiel, the lower the pitch of the note it produces.

Conventionally a glockenspiel is arranged so that the largest and lowest sounding bar is on the extreme left as

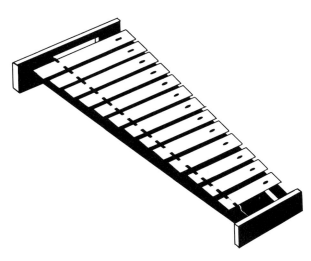

A soprano diatonic glockenspiel

10

The bars on most glockenspiels can be removed. This can be very useful if you are wanting to focus on only one or two sounds.

There are two types of glockenspiel: soprano and alto. The soprano has a smaller overall size and therefore has a higher pitch range than the alto glockenspiel.

Metallophone

A metallophone is constructed on the same principles as a glockenspiel, except that the bars are made of aluminium alloy. Metallophones are arranged and played in the same way as glockenspiels and can be of a diatonic or chromatic type. There are three types of metallophone: soprano (highest pitch range); alto (medium pitch range); bass (lowest pitch range). As before, the smaller the overall size of the instrument, the higher its pitch range. The vibration of notes on a metallophone lasts longer than those on the glockenspiel.

Xylophone

A xylophone is constructed on the same principles as the glockenspiel and metallophone. The bars on the xylophone, however, are made of wood – usually rosewood. It is again played with beaters, although the sound vibrates for a shorter period than in the case of the other two instruments. Xylophones can be diatonic or chromatic and are again arranged so that the smallest and highest-sounding bar is on the right. There are three types of xylophone – soprano, alto and bass – each larger and of a lower pitch range than the preceding one.

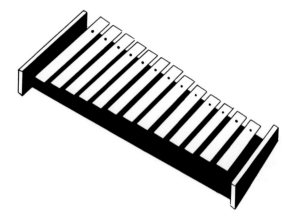

A soprano diatonic xylophone

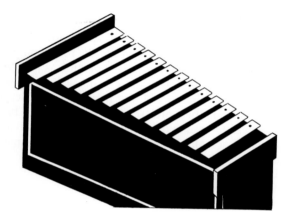

A bass diatonic metallophone

THE IMPORTANCE OF LISTENING

Listening is fundamental to any musical activity whether it be tuning an instrument, playing a scale evenly, rehearsing and practising a piece, improvising, composing, or presenting a performance. It also, of course, includes attending to performances by other people in live or recorded form. However, we need to be aware of certain problems and pitfalls where this type of activity is concerned.

Disadvantages of an information-based approach

There is a great danger of music becoming 'swamped in a welter of information about music, about composers, about instruments' (Salaman, 1982). This is particularly true where lessons devoted to listening to recorded performances are concerned. The disadvantage of such an approach is that it often detracts from, or becomes a substitute for, that direct live experience which is essential in music.

'Information may possibly, in some roundabout way,

motivate us to listen more attentively, but it will not in itself aid us in our perception of music. There is nothing that can be said that will equal the direct experience of sound.' (Paynter, 1982.)

Disadvantages of recorded music

Listening to music on record or tape is a very difficult activity and in many ways an unnatural one. If you go to any kind of concert, you do not usually sit there with your eyes closed, listening only to the sound. You watch the performers and audience and these visual stimuli can add to the interest and often help concentration and understanding. You, as the teacher, have the advantage of knowing the music and of having experienced live performances, as a listener/singer/instrumentalist. Therefore you are able, through experience and imagination, to compensate for the missing 'live' musical elements. This is less likely to be true of a class of young children.

11

Listening to music

In view of all this, there is a need to ensure that listening grows out of children's active exploration of music and is allied to performance activities and creative work.

Children who have tried to make up a story through their compositions are likely to be far more interested and know what to listen for when they come to hear a musical story produced by a professional composer. 'Their own activity in putting sounds together, or in taking decisions about points of interpretation or style of presentation, technically simple though it may be, will provide the all-important bridge between the reality of musical experience and the recorded sound.' (Paynter, 1982.)

'Those who have made up their own music are usually more discerning when they hear the music of others' (DES, 1985).

Allied to this is the need for focused, active, task-orientated listening. Whatever the style of music listened to, children are likely to gain far more if they are set tasks by being asked to listen *for* something, rather than letting the sounds wash over them.

Possible foci for listening

Below are a few examples, neither exhaustive nor definitive, which might help to prompt your own ideas.

● Distinguishing between: loud and soft, fast and slow, high and low sounds in the music.
● Deciding whether the music: runs, skips, walks, gallops.
● Identifying musical phrases (see glossary) and accents (see glossary).
● Identifying a well-known tune in the context of a larger work.
● Identifying a particular melodic progression when it is used as an ostinato (see glossary), for example.
● Identifying a rhythmic pattern (see glossary) when it appears or reappears in a composed work.
● Identifying different timbres (see glossary) of instruments/voices/combinations of these.
● Listening to the way a melody is used. Is it pitched high or low? Does it move slowly or is it played quickly? Does the mood of the melody change during successive appearances? If so, what causes it to change?
● Listening for recurrences of sections of music, i.e. attending to formal patterns.
● Where 'programme' music (i.e. descriptive music, or music which 'tells a story') is concerned, identifying when a particular event occurs.

NB   A great deal of music played to young children tends to fall into this last category. Remember to focus not so much on the story itself as on the *way* that it is told. This will ensure that the children concentrate on the music itself, rather than on peripheral elements.

What types of music should the children listen to?

It is quite clear from the National Curriculum Programme of Study that children should be exposed to as wide a range of musical styles as possible. You might have a particular liking for one type of music, but do not allow your preferences to dominate, since this could result in the limiting of your pupils' experiences as well as your own.

In this book, you will find suggestions for listening, together with advice on the types of elements to which the children's attention could be drawn in a specific piece of music. These activities are deliberately chosen so that they:

● relate closely to the practical performing and composing activities pursued;
● introduce children to a wide range of musical styles;
● help the children to begin to identify the particular characteristics of pieces of music from varying historical or cultural origins.

Resources for listening

The best way to build up a resource is to listen to a vast range of music. The references here are meant as no more than a starting point for such exploration. Simply relying on a narrow range of well-known works 'appropriate' for school will not do. Try to extend your own and your pupils' experiences as much as possible. Do not dismiss a particular piece of music because you think that the children will find it strange or obscure. Remember that their preferences and prejudices have not yet been formed to the same extent as your own and they might actually help you to hear more in a piece than you at first expected.

Listening to a piece only once or twice will not help children to become acquainted with it. As with stories, they need to build up familiarity by returning to the music several times, on their own as well as with others. It is therefore very important that within your school library there is a selection of cassettes and CDs and the facility – through listening stations, for example – for the children to listen to these on their own, in pairs and in small groups as well as in a full class.

Many schools play music to the children as they process into or out of assembly. This can have the effect of calming the children down and can contribute to the creation of an appropriate atmosphere for an act of collective worship. In many instances, teachers and headteachers also take this opportunity to extend the children's musical experiences by discussing the music briefly or by putting up a notice or display to indicate what the piece of music is and who wrote it. Such opportunities could be extended to include listening points for the children. For example, they could be asked to listen to the way that a particular instrument is used in the music or to how volume changes are employed. This approach could be developed into a theme for the week. This could take several forms, e.g.:

● Composer of the week: where several works by the same composer are played and a short information display is presented – possibly at the entrance to the assembly hall – giving biographical details and showing pictures of the composer;
● Instrument of the week: where several pieces

involving the same instrument are heard. Again this could be backed up with a display giving relevant information about the instrument and possibly including pictures of famous performers on the instrument;

• Music from the time of Henry VIII, or some other historical period, where a range of examples of several composers' music could be played;

• Storm music, where the children are given the opportunity to listen to the way that a particular idea has been explored by various composers. The accompanying display could be used to draw attention to the way that instrumental or volume contrasts are employed;

• Spirituals, where the children listen to further examples of spirituals, to extend their acquaintance with a genre that they have encountered in class. This could also apply to other genres, e.g. string quartets, symphonies, brass bands, etc.

The above list is presented as a spur to thought and is by no means exhaustive. The important point is to ensure that what is presented is seen as an extension of the musical activities pursued in class. They can also, of course, contribute to developments elsewhere in the curriculum. There are many ways of doing this.

• Contributions to English could be made by asking the children to write about or discuss the music which they have heard.
• Work in history can be enriched by listening to music from the specific period being investigated. (Music, it should be remembered, is an important artefact from any age.)
• Work in geography can be enhanced through exploring the origins of some of the music heard.
• The instrument of the week could be developed into further consideration of the science of sound production.

The reader no doubt will be able to extend this list and relate it to the particular context in which she/he is actually working. Remember that one of the most important sources of music to be listened to by large groups in assembly is that composed and/or performed by the children themselves!

COMPOSITION

Composing is probably the one area of the music curriculum which has struck greatest fear into the hearts of primary school teachers, regardless of whether or not they have had much experience of teaching music. As with singing, teachers often imagine that, unless they themselves are outstanding at this activity, they cannot begin to present it to their pupils. But how many teachers who pursue creative writing activities with their pupils have ever written a publishable poem or novel? How many teachers who pursue art with a class have ever exhibited a painting? In the areas of creative writing and art, teachers have long realised that the most important thing is to provide opportunities for children to investigate, experiment and try out ideas. The results of such endeavours are not to be judged against publicly acclaimed works but are to be viewed in relation to the emerging skills of pupils at that age or stage of development.

The same holds true of music. A child's composition at junior level might not be a symphony but, if it reflects an attempt to make patterns and shapes out of a range of sounds which the child has tried out, it could be a step on the way to producing one. As teachers gain more experience of helping children 'mess about with sounds', they will – as with visual arts and improvised drama – begin to build a set of expectations, be more realistic in their approach and, one hopes, become more confident about it.

In this book the emphasis will be on providing guidelines which will enable both teacher and pupils to work together on experimenting and creating in sound. You will soon come to see that the most important skills for this are not necessarily musical skills but those skills which you already possess as a teacher; the skills of organisation, presenting stimuli, prompting discussion, asking questions, and helping children to clarify their ideas and to comment constructively on their own and others' work.

Where should I hold the composition lesson?
By its very nature, music making must involve noise. This is particularly the case where composing is concerned, since children must have the opportunity to try out ideas and select, modify or reject them. It is highly unlikely that you will have sound-proofed accommodation in your school. To minimise the disruption to other activities, you might wish to use the school hall or a room set aside for such activities. In doing this, however, try to make sure that the activity does not become totally isolated from the other work being pursued in class. If no other accommodation is available you will simply have to use the classroom and possibly any additional spaces in the vicinity such as corridors or storage areas. You will of course need to ensure that your work is timetabled in such a way that it does not cause unnecessary disruption to quieter activities being pursued in neighbouring classrooms. On the other hand, do not let your concern for quieter activities lead to the abandonment of composition work since that would be an equal disruption and limitation of your pupils' experiences. With careful whole-school planning, composition can be conducted by each class with minimum disruption to others. This can be done in open-plan settings as much as in other types of schools.

13

How do I avoid unnecessary noise?

To ensure that music making is constructive and not simply chaos, it is essential to have good planning and organisation. The following points will help to ensure this:

1. Establish definite procedures for fetching and selecting instruments. In the early stages, or with younger classes, you might prefer to set out the instruments yourself in groups at various points in the room. You can then assign children to specific sets of instruments. Precisely which groupings of instruments you will use and how much freedom of choice you decide to give the pupils will vary according to their experience or stage of development and the nature of the project pursued.

2. Use a clear sign to start and stop the work. You might choose to use a cymbal crash or other loud noise. The danger is that this could be lost in the rest of the sounds being produced. On the other hand, children might be so engrossed in their work that they will not notice a visual sign. Decide on the best type of sign for the particular circumstances in which you find yourself.

3. When the instruments are not being played (e.g. when discussion is taking place), insist that they are put down carefully on the table or on the floor and not touched until further notice. (This also applies to beaters!)

4. When one group is performing, only allow that group to have instruments in their hands. The rest should be asked to put them down and leave them.

5. When the children are experimenting, encourage them to *listen* to each other and themselves and not indulge in random, aimless bashing of the instruments.

6. The children should talk to each other and not shout at each other during discussions.

7. The experimentation should occur in short bursts, otherwise the noise will build up to unbearable proportions.

8. Arrange the groups so that there is space between them. A group which has been asked to experiment with softer sounds should be positioned away from those whose improvisation is likely to involve louder sounds.

9. Even groups which have been asked to experiment with loud sounds should be encouraged to temper the volume during the practice session. They can always increase the volume when they are performing alone to the rest of the class.

Possible sequence for use in creative music making

There is no one 'right' way to sequence creative music making activities. What is presented below is one possible sequence which has been used very successfully, in a variety of contexts, by teachers with little previous experience of teaching music in general or composition in particular. It is presented here as a starting point which you can adapt, develop or reject as you gain more experience in this field. It is this sequence which lies at the basis of many of the projects which you find in this book.

Stage 1: Presentation of starting idea

Within each project, you will find a given starting idea. This might consist of a picture, word, rhythmic pattern or abstract idea. The first stage will be for you to discuss this with the children. Possible questions and avenues of enquiry are suggested at each stage in the book. When you and the class have had sufficient experience of composing, you might ask a child to lead the discussion at this point.

It is important that this first stage should not be too long (about 5 minutes should be sufficient), otherwise the active part of the lesson will be unnecessarily curtailed.

Stage 2: Free exploration by groups

At this point each group begins to experiment with the instruments which they have been given. The children will be primarily concerned with finding out what kinds of sound their particular instruments can produce. Then gradually they will begin to relate them to the demands of the specific project set.

During this stage, your involvement need be no more than making sure that any organisational problems are sorted out. You could also use this stage to give children practice in stopping and starting in response to the given signal. There should be no need for you to be involved with any specific group at this point. Your job is to create the context in which the children can pursue their own explorations.

After approximately 5 minutes, stop the children. Tell them that up until now they have been trying out sounds and a few ideas. They will no doubt have been changing them and adapting them as they do so. Now what they must do is to decide which ideas they want to use and practise putting those into a particular order ready for performance to the rest of the class. Tell them that it does not matter whether the idea is a very short one. The important thing is that they should, as a group, know what they intend to do.

Give them all a further 5–6 minutes to do this.

Stage 3: Presenting of initial ideas by groups to the whole class

At this point invite one of the groups to present its ideas to the rest of the class. Ask them to play their ideas twice. The listeners will also have the chance to absorb what they are hearing. It is essential at this stage that both the pupils and you are seen to be listening intently to what is being performed. Quite often children will wade into a piece without waiting for a complete silence before starting. Similarly they will begin to talk or make extraneous movements or sounds immediately after the last note has been sounded. Encourage them and give them practice in putting a 'frame of concentrated silence' around the work that is being presented for comment.

When the excerpt has been heard twice ask the rest of the class 'What do you like about this piece of music?' That is a very different question from asking 'Do you like this piece of music?' The first allows for the presentation and exploration of reasons and ideas. The second invites no more than a one word answer. The children will comment on a range of aspects at this stage.

When this has been exhausted, ask the performers themselves whether there are any further aspects of their work which they like. Now ask them: 'How do you think your piece could be made better or made different?' When the group itself has exhausted its own ideas, ask the rest of the class what they feel could be changed or made better. The fact that the starting point of the questioning has been positive will mean that no one will feel threatened either by presenting or receiving criticism in this way. As children offer their ideas, ask them to clarify what they mean or possibly demonstrate alternative approaches.

Do not worry if apparently contradictory ideas have been suggested within or from outside the group. Ask the children to explore all the suggestions and then decide which they prefer. Experience of working with vast numbers of children suggests that certain traits will emerge at this stage in the proceedings:

• Very often a group of children will all play simultaneously throughout the piece.
• Very often the piece will have no silences.
• Quite often the children will have difficulty in starting and stopping the piece.
• There will be a tendency for some groups to give oral instructions to each other mid-performance.

Through questioning, encourage the children to discover these traits for themselves, then ask them how they might overcome the problems. They will often suggest that each member of the group could come in one after the other until everyone is playing. Then they could stop playing one after the other – possibly in reverse order. Later this could be developed to suggesting that varying groups of children could play at different times. For example, in a group of five players, you might have performers playing as follows:

1, 2, 1 and 2 together, 3, 4, 3 and 4 together, 3, 4 and 5 together, all together, 1 and 2 together, 1 alone to finish. This of course is only one amongst a myriad of possibilities that present themselves.

In the case of starting and stopping the children often suggest counting in loudly or giving some other form of oral instructions. Through discussion, encourage them to see the disadvantages of having spoken indications. How therefore might they indicate starts and stops soundlessly? Encourage them to find gestures to help themselves and each other.

It should be clear by now that the approach being advocated is one of identifying a problem and finding a range of possible solutions through discussion. Groups which have not yet performed will have been imagining other possibilities for their own pieces. Now ask all groups to go back to their original ideas and modify them in the light of what has already been discussed. At the end of this stage, recap on the ideas which have been suggested and ask the group to try out the ideas and any others which might suggest themselves during further exploration.

Stage 4: Working on the ideas suggested by the discussion during Stage 3 (group work)
During this stage each group will:

• experiment with the ideas presented during discussion;
• discuss each of the ideas and suggest further possibilities to each other;
• revise the new ideas as a result of the discussion;
• decide which ideas they prefer and how they wish to put them together;
• rehearse the new ideas ready for performance to the rest of the class.

All the above will be interspersed with appraisal by the group, and by the teacher in conjunction with the group and the whole class.

Stage 5: Further presentation and discussion of reworked ideas (group and whole class activity).
This stage will be very similar to stage 3. This time, however, start by listening to groups which you have not heard hitherto. Ally this with listening to a reworking of a piece already heard. This stage will vary in length according to the children's age, experience, time availability and the ultimate aim of the project.

Final presentation
Ultimately the stages outlined above will result in a final presentation by each group to the whole class. After constantly working, reworking and discussing their piece children will rarely have difficulty in remembering what they have to perform. It is amazing that they can even remember what they have to do over several weeks. You might, however, wish to notate the piece or tape record it. Suggestions on how this might be done will be made elsewhere in this book.

Discussing emerging compositions
In discussing their own and others' work, encourage the children to ask the following types of questions which will focus on a particular musical concept.

Volume
What would happen if the music was louder or softer? What would happen if the music suddenly became loud or suddenly became soft? What would happen if the music became gradually louder or gradually softer?

Tempo
How would the music sound if it was played more slowly? How would it sound if it was played more quickly? What would happen if it suddenly speeded up or suddenly slowed down? What would happen if it gradually became faster or slower?

Timbre/tone colour
How would a particular piece of the music sound if it was played on a different instrument? What would the effect be if the instrument was played in a different way (e.g. if it were stroked instead of hit or if it were tapped instead of shaken?)

Texture
What would happen if the music had different combinations of instruments, e.g. one instrument, all

instruments; a set of three instruments followed by a set of four or two instruments?

Register
Would the tune sound better if it was played at a higher or lower pitch?

Balance
What would happen if one instrument played more loudly or more softly than another?

Rhythm
Could the pattern of the rhythm be changed or made more interesting? Could the rhythm of one musical idea be transferred to another musical idea?

Form
How could the overall shape of the music be changed? What would the effect be? How could the shape be made more varied without the piece sounding like a combination of disjointed ideas?

At first, the children could address one or more of these questions separately. Later, however, they could ask themselves and each other how the music could be varied and made more interesting through a combination of the above ideas.

Whatever the questions asked, the answer can only be found by testing out and listening to the effect. Music should be evaluated on the basis of what is heard, not on the basis of some abstract theory of what is right or wrong.

How can a composition be notated?
In this book, you will find a variety of ways of notating compositions. Where the children are involved in mak-

ing up melodies, using specific pitches, they will be given the opportunity to write down their melodies using letter names. You will find examples of this in Activities 52, 62 and 79 and on Copymasters 65, 74 and 88.

In some instances, the sounds which the children use in their compositions cannot be precisely defined in this way. In those cases, the children will use pictures or symbols to represent their ideas. Examples of the use of what is known as 'graphic notation' may be found in Activities 5, 37, 43 and 65 and on Copymasters 4, 42, 49 and 76.

Why should a composition be notated?
There are two main reasons for notating compositions: the first is to ensure that the ideas contained in them are preserved; the second is to enable others to reproduce the music. In many instances, where the children need to remember what the music is like so that they can extend it further, a tape recording will be sufficient. The important point in such cases is to ensure that the children are given sufficient practice in using the tape recorder to enable them to use it independently and at the time when it is most crucial for them.

In other instances, the children will be given the opportunity to write down their music, in one form or another. You will notice that, in those cases, they will be urged not only to play back their own ideas but also to play each other's music. In this way, they will learn to be accurate and precise in their notation. It will also ensure that the notation activity is given meaning and that it relates to, and supports, the practical activity, rather than becoming a discrete activity pursued as an end in itself.

REFERENCES

Salaman, W., 1982, *Living School Music*, Cambridge University Press.

Paynter, J., 1982, *Music in the Secondary School Curriculum*, Cambridge University Press.

DES, 1985, *Curriculum Matters 4: Music from 5 to 16*.

1. MISTER FROG'S WEDDING

2. He rode up to Miss Mousie's door
   Ah hum! Ah hum!
   He rode up to Miss Mousie's door,
   He gave three taps and stamped on the floor
   Ah hum! Ah hum!

3. He fell down upon his knee
   Ah hum! Ah hum!
   He fell down upon his knee.
   'Miss Mouse,' he said, 'Will you marry me?'
   Ah hum! Ah hum!

4. Mister Frog was dressed in green
   Ah hum! Ah hum!
   Mister Frog was dressed in green
   By his side Miss Mouse looked like a queen
   Ah hum! Ah hum!

5. The chief guest was the bumblebee
   Ah hum! Ah hum!
   The chief guest was the bumblebee
   He played his fiddle upon his knee
   Ah hum! Ah hum!

6. They went away on their honeymoon
   Ah hum! Ah hum!
   They went away on their honeymoon
   We hope to see them both back soon
   Ah hum! Ah hum!

Purpose
To give the children the experience of singing a song consisting of a verse and a chorus; to give them practice in moving in time to the underlying beat of a song and in adding a simple accompaniment to it; to give them experience of singing individually or in small groups as well as in a full class group.

Resources
Cassette: side 1, activity 1
Copymaster 1
Chime bars: F C F'
Space for movement

Presentation
Using the cassette and the ideas included in the introduction to this book, teach the children the following song.

Starting note: F
Count in: 1 2 1 2

Mr Frog's Wedding

1. Frog went a-courting he did ride
   Ah hum! Ah hum!
   Frog went a-courting he did ride,
   With sword and pistol by his side
   Ah hum! Ah hum!

When they can sing it fairly confidently, ask the children to sing the first verse, this time pretending to ride a horse as they do so and moving in time with the beat of the music. From here you can progress to having one child or a small group of children singing the verse, while the rest join in with the 'Ah hum' of the chorus. You could then discuss with the children ways of acting out the rest of the song. You could also involve them in extending the song by adding their own verses as more and more curious wedding guests arrive.

You could now extend the activity by asking two children to play the instrumental accompaniment, using **Copymaster 1**. The first child should play the lower sounding F on the first beat of every bar. The second child should play the following pattern in time to the beat:

1	2
High F	C
(r.h.)	(l.h.)

In all the copymasters, this sign { ♪ } indicates that the left hand beater is to be used while this sign { ◯ }

shows that the right hand is to be used. It is important that children should be encouraged to use two beaters as this will ultimately enable them to play far more complicated music than is possible with only one beater.

The accompaniment pattern should be played regularly throughout the piece. Make sure that the children playing the instruments keep singing, otherwise they will have difficulty in keeping in time with the others. Also remember that the accompaniment should not be allowed to drown the singing.

Extension
There are many versions of this song, both in Britain and America. Some versions have many verses. You could, if you wished, invite the children to add further verses, or invent additional verses yourself so that the story and the activity is extended.

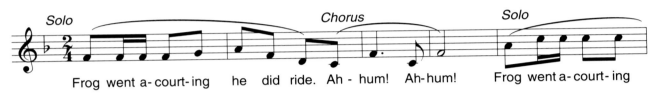

2. BLOW THE MAN DOWN

Purpose
To give the children further experience of moving to the underlying beat and accents of a song; to give them further experience of performing a song based on a solo–chorus pattern and of adding a simple accompaniment to it.

Resources
Cassette: side 1, activity 2
Copymaster 2
Bass xylophone/metallophone with the notes C and G highlighted. If such instruments are not available, use chime bars.
Space for movement

Background information
In days gone by, sailors had none of the computers and modern technology which are found on ships nowadays and all the work had to be done by hand. This included raising and lowering the anchor, hoisting the sails and loading and unloading the cargo. Most of these jobs were too heavy for one man to perform, and whole gangs of men worked together. If a sail was to be raised properly and the anchor to be raised smoothly, it was essential that all the men working on the task moved exactly together. To help with this, they often sang songs and timed their movements with the main beats and words of the song. These songs would also have been a useful form of entertainment and would have helped while away the time and make what must have been a tedious task a little more bearable. To increase the fun, the words of the songs were often ridiculous and the sailors would take turns in making up new and humorous verses. Additional verses can be contributed by individual pupils or groups.

Presentation
With the aid of the cassette and the suggestions included in the introduction to this book, teach the children the following song.

Starting note: G
Count in: 1 2 1 2

Blow the Man Down

1. Solo	Blow the man down, bullies, blow the man down
	Chorus	Weigh heigh blow the man down

Solo	Blow the man down, bullies, blow him away
Chorus	Give me some time to blow the man down
2. Solo	As I was a walking down Paradise Street
Chorus	Weigh heigh blow the man down
Solo	A pretty young damsel I did chance to meet
Chorus	Give me some time to blow the man down
3. Solo	I asked her to sail with me over the sea
Chorus	Weigh heigh blow the man down
Solo	She said that right there was where she'd like to be
Chorus	Give me some time to blow the man down
4. Solo	I bad her farewell as we sailed from the shore
Chorus	Weigh heigh blow the man down
Solo	And now I shall never see her no more
Chorus	Give me some time to blow the man down

Once the children have learnt to perform it with a fair degree of confidence, ask them to mime movements associated with raising and lowering the anchor and hauling on ropes. Then give them the opportunity to perform these in time to the strong beats in the music as they sing the song through again.

Extension
From here you can progress to adding the accompaniment indicated on **Copymaster 2**, again on the first, accented beats of each bar. Start by adding this accompaniment yourself. Then invite some of the children to take turns in playing it as they and the rest of the class sing the song. Remember that when you see this sign { ↗ } the left-hand beater should be used and that when you see this sign { ↘ } you should use the right-hand beater.

Blow the man down bul-lies blow the man down Weigh heigh blow the man down.

Blow the man down bul-lies blow him a-way Give me some time to blow the man down.

3. TIMBRE GAME

Purpose
To help develop the children's skill in identifying specific instruments from their sounds.

Resources
An instrument per child in the group. It will be best if, at first, each child has a different type of instrument from the others.
Cassette: side 1, activity 3
Copymaster 3

Presentation
Arrange the children in a circle, with one child blindfolded and sitting in the centre of the circle. Give each child in the circle an instrument. Select one instrument and say its name, e.g. tambourine. Do not, however, make a sound with the instrument. At a sign from you, all the children begin to play their instruments together. The blindfolded child wanders around the circle until she or he identifies the instrument being played. If the correct instrument is identified, that

19

player changes places with the blindfolded child and the game starts again, this time with a different instrument being named. When they have had sufficient practice at this game, invite the children themselves to lead the activity and select the instrument to be identified.

To perform this activity successfully, the children must have been given the opportunity to acquaint themselves with the sounds which each instrument makes. It might be helpful to draw on some of the activities in *Blueprints: Music Key Stage 1* to help you with this.

Extension

This time include more than one example of each instrument in the circle. The blindfolded child will then have to identify all the instruments of the given type being played.

This can be followed up with the game of 'I Hear With My Musical Ear', using the copymaster and the cassette track indicated.

The answers to this game are as follows:

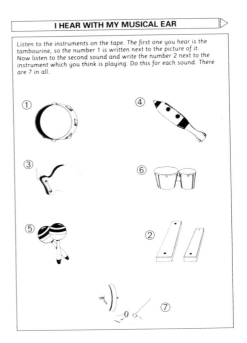

I HEAR WITH MY MUSICAL EAR

Listen to the instruments on the tape. The first one you hear is the tambourine, so the number 1 is written next to the picture of it. Now listen to the second sound and write the number 2 next to the instrument which you think is playing. Do this for each sound. There are 7 in all.

4. I'M REACHING HIGH, HIGH, HIGH

Purpose

To enable the children to develop the concept of pitch through identifying high and low sounds and responding to them with appropriate movements; to give them practice in converting signs into sounds and sounds into signs in preparation for later work on reading and writing pitch notation.

Resources

Space for movement
Two chime bars: D and D' (a higher pitched chime bar stamped with the same letter).
A high surface, e.g. table top or piano top and a low surface, e.g. the floor.
Cassette: side 1, activity 4

Presentation

Using the cassette and the suggestions in the introduction to the book, teach the children the following song.
Starting note: A
Count in: 1 2 3 4 1 2 3

I'm Reaching High High High

I'm reaching high high high
I'm bending right down low
I'm wondering where where where
Should I go go go
I'm creeping up up up
From the floor floor floor
I'm reaching high
I'm reaching high
I'm bending low.

When the children can sing it fairly confidently, ask them to arrange themselves in spaces around the room. Now, as they sing, they should reach up high on the words 'high, high, high' and crouch down low on the words 'low, low, low'. Help them to find ways of making a variety of shapes as they do so. Then, as they sing, play the high D' on the words 'high, high, high' and the low D on the words 'low, low, low'. If there are children who can manage to do this, ask them to take turns in playing the accompaniment. Make sure, however, that as they do so, these children keep singing, otherwise they will find difficulty in synchronising the chime bar sounds with the sung sounds.

Now ask the children to spread themselves around the room facing you. Show them that on a higher surface you have placed the higher sounding chime bar from the set and that on the floor you have placed the lower sounding bar. Tell them that as you play the high sound they should reach up high and as you play the low sound they should crouch down low. Ask them to make sure that each time they stretch or crouch, they produce a different and interesting shape with their bodies. Play this game a few times, until most of the class can do it confidently.

From here you can progress to playing the game with the children facing away from you so that they now have to rely on the sound rather than the visual clues to decide on the pitch of the notes. To make sure that they are developing their own listening skills and not simply copying from their class-mates, ask them to keep their eyes closed as they do so.

Now sit the class in a semi-circle and ask three children to stand in a row facing the class. In front of the children place the chime bars – the low sounding D on the left, the high sounding D on the right. Ask each child who is facing the class to make a shape – high or low. Discuss the height of the shapes with the children.

If the first shape is a high shape, play the high chime bar. If the next one is low, play the low sounding chime bar and so on.

Let various children take turns in making the shapes and in playing them on the chime bars. When they can do this, play a series of notes on the chime bars, e.g. high high low and ask three children to arrange themselves into equivalent shapes. By pursuing such activities, the children will be developing the skills of converting signs into sounds and sounds into signs – the prerequisites of reading and writing music.

Extension
As the children gain confidence in pursuing this activity, the number of sounds which have to be converted into shapes or the number of shapes to be converted into sounds can be extended. The numbers can also be varied to provide appropriate challenges for children of varying abilities and experiences in the class.

I'm rea-ching high   high   high. I'm ben-ding   right   down   low. I'm wonder-ing

where   where where___   should I   go___   go___   go I'm cree-ping up   up   up___   from the

floor   floor   floor I'm rea-ching high___   I'm rea-ching high___   I'm ben-ding   low.___

5. STORM AT SEA

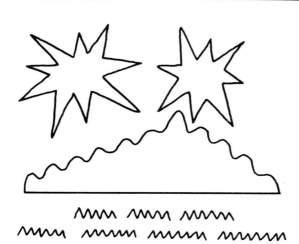

Purpose
To give the children the opportunity to improvise and perform a piece based on a graphic score.

Resources
Copymaster 4
A variety of pitched and unpitched instruments
Tape recorder

Presentation
Discuss **Copymaster 4** with the children. Explain to them that this is what is known as a graphic score. The pictures give a general idea of the types of sounds that are to be produced but it is up to them to work out precisely which sounds should be used for each symbol. Ask individuals to take specific symbols and to experi-

ment with producing sounds to correspond to them. Invite the children to play the sounds to each other and to discuss and refine them. When this has been done, divide the children into groups to produce their own improvisations. Use the approach suggested in the introduction to help the class develop their ideas, to criticise their own and each others' work and to arrive at a final version which can then be recorded on tape if they so wish.

Extension

When completed, the tape or live performance could be presented to others in the school, as part of an assembly theme, for example. Alternatively, the tapes could be part of a sound folio built up by the class and made available for listening to the children themselves or to visitors to the classroom.

6. HIGH, MIDDLE & LOW SOUNDS ▶

Purpose

To give the children practice in identifying high-, middle- and low-pitched sounds and in converting sounds into signs and signs into sounds.

Resources

Space for movement
Three chime bars of different pitches

Starting note: G
Count in: 1 2 1 2

Presentation

You could start by recapping Activity 4 above, particularly the extension section. Now teach them the following song. When they can sing it confidently, add the chime bar accompaniment. Then, invite individual children to take over from you.

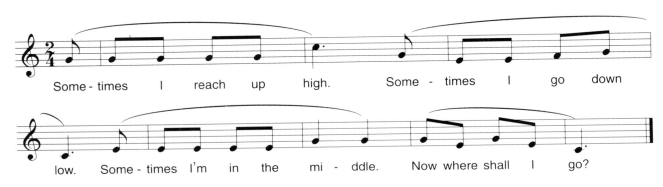

Some - times I reach up high. Some - times I go down low. Some - times I'm in the mi - ddle. Now where shall I go?

Identifying high, low and middle pitch sounds

As before, arrange the children into a semicircle and ask three children to face them. Arrange the three chime bars used in the song so that, viewed from left to right by the majority of the pupils, they will look as follows:

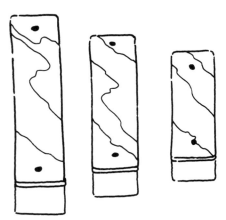

As in the extension to Activity 4, you can now pursue a reading activity where the three children make a shape each (high, middle or low) to be converted into the appropriate pitch equivalent on the chime bars. Then develop this into a notation activity, where you play a sequence of notes and ask the children to arrange themselves, from left to right, into the appropriate sequence of shapes.

You can now vary the patterns and the number of children and sounds involved to give the children further experiences of converting sounds into signs and signs into sounds. Here again, the complexity of the task can be varied to meet the individual needs of the pupils in the class.

It is not intended that all the activities described here should be pursued all in one go. Rather, they provide variations on a theme to which you can return at varying intervals, to give pupils practice and further challenges in relation to the activity.

7. RHYTHM CLAPPING

Purpose

To introduce the children to the basis of rhythmic notation by enabling them to perform, hear and read sounds of differing lengths.

Resources

Cassette: side 1, activity 7
Space for movement
Copymaster 5

Presentation

Start by listening to the examples on the tape and asking the children to reproduce the patterns they hear. Ask the children to march around the room as they chant these words:

I march
You march
We march
They march
All go
March march
Round the
Big room

Now ask them to repeat this activity, this time clapping on every word.

When they have done this, draw their attention to the fact that there is one word and one clap to each foot movement.

Now ask them to chant this verse, again marching round the room as they do so:

Why do el-e- phants like sti-cky buns? Eh?
　1　2 1　　2　 1　2　 　1　　2

Once more, ask them to clap the rhythm of the words as they march. This time, they will notice that in most cases there is one clap to a foot beat. But on 'e-le' and 'sti-cky', there are two sounds to a foot beat each time.

Here are further examples which include two sounds per foot beat which you and the children can perform by clapping the word rhythm while marching around.

Where has my little
Di- no -saur gone to?

Or -an -ges and
le -mons
say the bells of Saint
Cle-ments

Lit-tle mouse lit-tle mouse
May we come to see your house?

Explain to the children that you can illustrate this by the use of large or small pictures of objects. Show them the examples on the Copymaster. Now ask them to clap these rhythms, following the pictures. Remind them to march on the spot and to make only one clap on a foot beat when there is only one picture.

When they have attempted the clapping, ask them to listen to the same patterns being performed on the tape, in order to compare their own performance and correct it if necessary. Obviously, the lesson will run far more smoothly if you have listened to and memorised these patterns before embarking on the activity with the children.

Like many activities in this book, do not expect to be able to cover this in one go. You will need to present it gradually and return to it from time to time for the sake of consolidation. If you find that some children have difficulty grasping these ideas, go back to the sections on rhythm work in *Blueprints: Music Key Stage 1* and work through those sections again.

8. HOW ARE SOUNDS PRODUCED?

Purpose
To help children understand that sounds can be produced in a variety of different ways.

Resources
Copymaster 6

Presentation
Use **Copymaster 6** as a basis for a discussion of how sounds are produced. Then help the children to apply their understanding by making lists and drawing pictures of all the instruments which are played by blowing, banging and scraping.

9. OK YOU GUYS!

Purpose
To give the children further experience of marking the beats and accents of a song through movement; to give them further practice in performing contrasts of volume; to enable them to identify two-beat metres and to indicate this through movement.

Resources
Cassette: side 1, activity 9
Space for movement

Presentation
Using the cassette and the suggestions included at the beginning of this book, teach the children to sing the following song:

Starting note: C
Count in: 1 2 1 2

OK You Guys!

O.K. 1	you guys 2	make a 1	ring 2	'Cos we're 1	gonna 2	dance and 1	sing 2
Shift to the 1	left 2	Shift to the 1	right 2	Just keep 1	shiftin' 2	day and 1	night 2
Now let's 1	hear it 2	Give a 1	clap A 2	slap and 1	clap and 2	not a 1	tap 2
Slap and 1	clap 2	Slap and 1	clap A 2	slap and 1	clap and 2	not a 1	tap 2
Stamp your 1	foot and 2	move a- 1	round 2	C'mon let's 1	hear it 2	Stamp that 1	ground 2
Stamp and 1	clap 2	Stamp and 1	clap 2	Don't just 1	give a 2	measly 1	tap 2

24

When they can perform the song fairly accurately, focus on singing the last line (last four bars) more softly than the preceding section, so that it gives the effect of an echo. Now ask the children to sit in a circle and to mark the beat by tapping gently on their laps. This can then be developed to a point where the children mark the beats with a loud knee slap followed by a softer hand clap. Alternatively, invite them to move around the room, stepping in time to the beat of the music. From here they can progress to stamping their left feet on the beats marked 1 and also clapping at the same time. This will produce an even more accented sound.

When they can do either or both sets of activities confidently, explain to the children that the beats are grouped into groups of 2, with the first one in each group being accented with the knee slap.

Extension

This activity can be extended into a dance. To do this, arrange the children in two equal lines facing each

other. The children in each line hold hands with their neighbours in that line. Now teach them the following sequence of activities to be performed as they sing:

Bars 1 and 2: The children in each line move to their left, stepping in time to the beat.
Bars 3 and 4: The children in each line move to the right, again stepping in time to the beat.
Bars 5 and 6: Holding their neighbours' hands, the children in each line take four steps forward to meet the children in the other line.
Bars 7 and 8: Both lines take four steps back to their original positions.
Bars 9 and 10: Without holding hands the children in each line take four steps forward to meet their counterparts in the other line.
Bars 11 and 12: Each child takes two steps forward, passing to the left of the child facing him/her. Then on the last two steps they all turn round so that they are now once again facing each other but this time from opposite sides.

O. K.   you guys   make a   ring,   'Cos we're   go - nna   dance and   sing.

Shift   to   the left.   Shift   to   the right.   Just keep   shif - tin'   day and   night.

Shift   to   the left.   Shift   to   the right.   Just keep   shif - tin'   day and   night.

10. SKIP TO MY LOU

Purpose

To give the children further experience of performing a song based on a verse–chorus pattern; singing individually or in small groups as well as in a full class group; moving in time to the beats and accents of a song; adding a simple instrumental accompaniment to the song learnt; and of devising new words and accompanying movements for the tune.

Resources

Cassette: side 1, activity 10
Chime bars F and C
Tambour/drum/tambourine
Space for movement
Copymaster 7

Presentation

Using the cassette and the suggestions included in the

introduction to this book, teach the children the following song.

Starting note: A
Count in: 1 2 1 2

Skip to my Lou

1. Chorus: Skip skip skip to my Lou (3 times)
              Skip to my Lou my darling
   Solo: Lost my partner, what shall I do? (3 times)
              Skip to my Lou my darling

2. Chorus: Hop hop hop to my Lou (3 times)
              Hop to my Lou my darling
   Solo: I'll never find another as pretty as you (3 times)
              Hop to my Lou my darling

3. Chorus: Jump, jump, jump to my Lou (3 times)
              Jump to my Lou my darling
   Solo: Little red wagon painted blue (3 times)
              Jump to my Lou my darling

4. Chorus: Stamp, stamp, stamp to my Lou (3 times)
              Stamp to my Lou my darling
   Solo: Cows in the meadow, Moo, Moo, Moo! (3 times)
              Stamp to my Lou my darling

When they can sing the tune fairly confidently, divide the children into two groups: the first half to sing the verse and the second half to sing the chorus. Draw their attention to the fact that, unlike the previous songs of this type, this song starts with the chorus and not with the solo. Later, you could invite individuals or small groups to sing the verse as a solo/duet/trio etc. while the rest of the class sings the chorus.

From here, you can progress to asking the children to tap out the beat of the song on their laps as they sing it. You might wish to reinforce this by tapping it out gently on a tambour, tambourine, drum or any other unpitched percussion instrument available. To reinforce the feel of the underlying beat further, you could ask the children to make a large circle and, holding hands, to step in time to the beat as they sing, moving first in one direction then the other.

The next stage involves the children in marking the accented beats in the music through movement. To do this, they should find spaces for themselves around the room and this time, as they sing, they should make the appropriate movement suggested by the words (skip, jump, hop etc) on the first beat of every bar.

You are now ready to add the instrumental accompaniment to the song. You could start by adding this yourself, using **Copymaster 7**. Make sure that, as you play, you arrange the chime bars as indicated and that you use two beaters: the left hand beater for C and the right hand beater for F. At a later point, you could invite individual children to play the accompaniment.

When they have mastered the song as it stands, invite individual children to sing the verse and to make up new movements, accompanied by the appropriate gesture, as they sing. The chorus will then have to imitate these improvised movements.

26

11. CONTRASTING TIMBRES: PERFORMANCE AND COMPOSITION ACTIVITIES

Purpose
To give the children the opportunity to experiment with sounds of varying timbres and volumes and to use these to create a composition of their own.

Resources
Copymaster 8

Presentation
Work through **Copymaster 8** with the children. This should be self-explanatory.

12. RHYTHM DEVILS

Purpose
To develop the children's powers of concentration and enable them to keep a regular beat, even when other patterns are being played simultaneously. Through this, to prepare the children for future ensemble performance activities.

Resources
Metronome
Tambour
Copymaster 9
An instrument per child
Space for movement

Presentation
The children sit or stand in two rows, facing each other. Begin to beat out a slow, steady and regular beat on a woodblock. Alternatively, you could set a metronome going. Remember not to let the beat be too quick,

otherwise the children will find the activity too difficult. Ask the children to tap out the beat at the same time as you.

When they can do this, beat out groups of five beats and ask the children to say 'one' and 'five' but to think the intervening numbers. The next step is to ask them not to tap except when they say number one or number five. When they have mastered this, try the same activity, this time asking them to say and tap numbers one and three only.

Now divide them into two groups. Group A says and claps beats one and five while group B says and claps beats one and three.

When they can do this, invite one child to choose an instrument and to make up an entirely separate idea on that instrument. This time, as groups A and B perform their respective patterns, the Rhythm Devil tries to put them off by playing against them.

Extension
This activity could be extended by

● increasing the number of groups involved;
● increasing the number of Rhythm Devils;
● varying the length of the beat patterns to 4 or 6 or 7 and asking the children to play on different instruments;
● involving the pupils in playing on instruments rather than just clapping;
● through various combinations of the above activities.

You could also use **Copymaster 9**. Divide the class into four groups. Each group should follow one of the lines marked with a letter and play on the beats marked with crosses. When they have mastered this, the children could make up and perform their own patterns, using the blank beat square at the foot of the copymaster page.

Again remember that you can return to these activities from time to time, varying them on each occasion. You could also use the variations to cater for groups of different abilities and experience within your

13. VOICE SQUARES

Resources
Chalk board/OHP
Copymaster 10

Presentation
Divide the board into 16 squares as indicated on the copymaster. Tell the children that each square represents a beat. Invite them to suggest vocal sounds which could be entered on some beats and write these accordingly. Start by ensuring that each sound effect is different. Keep some squares empty, so that the eventual performance will involve silences as well as sounds. Tap a steady rhythm with your foot or using a metronome and point to each square in turn. The children should then say the sounds on the appropriate beats.

Extension
Divide the class into two groups and perform the piece as a canon. The second group enters as the first group performs square/beat 9.

As well as indicating sounds the children could indicate varying volumes for each sound. Large letters could be used for loud sounds and smaller ones for softer sounds. Alternatively, you could use different colours to indicate varying volumes. After each rendering consider how the effects could be improved or altered by changing the volume or length of the sounds.

Purpose
To give the children further experiences of group improvisation and to involve them in elementary notation activities

14. MAINTAINING AND TRANSFERRING THE BEAT

Purpose
To give the children practice in maintaining and transferring a regular beat pattern.

Resources
Cassette: side 1, activity 14

Presentation
Using the cassette and the suggestions in the introduction to this book, teach the children the following song:

Starting note: C
Count in: 1 2 1 2

Take the	beat and	pass it	round	Ne ver	let it	hit the	ground—
1	2	1	2	1	2	1	2
A to	B and	B to	C and	C to	D and	D to	E
1	2	1	2	1	2	1	2
Then be-	gin to	throw it	round	Till your	own –	letter's–	found—
1	2	1	2	1	2	1	2

A	to	G	or	F	to	E	or	D	to	B	and	G	to	E
1		2		1		2		1		2		1		2
Take the		beat and		pass it		round		Never		let it		hit———		
1		2		1		2		1		2		1		2
												f		

———————		the	ground———	———————	
1		2	1		2

As they sing the song, ask the children to tap gently on their laps in time to the underlying pulse of the music. When they can perform it confidently, arrange the children in a circle and give each child a letter name from A to G. Now perform the song again. When you get to the second line, children with the letter name A should sing 'A to B'; children with the letter name B should sing 'B to C' and so on. The important point is that no child should be late coming in.

Extension
Repeat the song but this time let the children make up their own paths by calling out letters in random order.

15. COPYING AND ADDING

Purpose
To give children further practice in maintaining and transferring beats and to enable them to mark regular beat patterns with a variety and combination of gestures.

Resources
Metronome and/or tambour
Cassette: side 1, activity 15

Presentation

Arrange the children in a circle. Begin by tapping out a steady beat on a tambour, in time to the metronome if you are using one. Make sure that the beat is not too fast. Ask the children to tap out a steady beat on their laps in time with you as you count regularly 1-2, 1-2. Now perform the following pattern in time to the regular beat and ask the children to copy you, again in time:

Teacher: Tap Tap Clap Clap
                  1   2   1   2

Children   Tap Tap Clap Clap
                  1   2   1   2

Teacher: Tap Tap Click Click
                  1   2   1   2

Children: Tap Tap Click Click
                  1   2   1   2

Teacher: Tap Tap Ankle Ankle
                           tap   tap
                  1   2   1   2

Children: Tap Tap Ankle Ankle
                           tap   tap
                  1   2   1   2

Remember that, when you and the children are performing this, the underlying beat must be kept regular.

When you have performed this activity, repeat it. This time use new patterns, suggested by yourself or the children over the beat.

The next stage is to send patterns around the circle. Once again, arrange the children in a circle and ask them all to keep a steady beat of 1-2, 1-2 by beating gently on their laps, in time with each other. Once the beat is being maintained, produce a pattern as before (e.g. pat pat, clap clap). This time, the child on your right should repeat it exactly as you produced it and then add her or his own version (e.g. pat pat clap clap clap clap click click). The next child on the right should now repeat the variation and add a further variation (e.g. clap clap click click click click slap slap). Thus, each child in turn takes the last idea from the left, repeats it and adds a variation of it until the turn comes back to the teacher. When it is not their turn, the

children should keep the underlying pulse going by tapping gently in time with the rest of the class.

It is best to start this activity with small groups of children and then build up the size of the groups gradually as the children grasp what is required of them. Plenty of practice in copying ideas from you before embarking on the first 'passing round' will also help make the activity more successful.

Ask the children to sing the song as they keep the beat going.

Extension 1

When the children have mastered this activity, vary it by sending the pattern around in a different direction. You could also invite individual children to start the activity. Once they can do this, you could progress to having more than one circle performing at one time.

Extension 2

Repeat the above activity. Before starting, however, give each child in the circle a letter. This time, ask each child to play the pattern twice, e.g. Tap Tap Clap Clap Tap Tap Clap Clap. As the repeat is being performed, the child should announce the letter of the child who is to follow, e.g.

Child A   'B!'
          Tap Tap Clap Clap Tap Tap Clap Clap
            1   2   1   2   1   2   1   2

Child B   'F!'
          Tap Tap Clap Clap Tap Tap Click Click
            1   2   1   2   1   2   1   2

Child F   'H!'
          Tap Tap Click Click Tap Tap Ankle Ankle
            1   2   1   2   1   2   1   2

You could develop this into a game where, if a child is not in on time, she or he is out. The last one in is the winner. As before, this activity is best tried with a small group at first. Also, in common with many of the activities in this book, you will need to return to it several times to give children practice and the opportunity to develop their skills further each time.

16. TALLIS'S CANON ▶

Purpose

To teach the children the well-known tune by Thomas Tallis; to enable them to sing it as a canon and to provide a simple accompaniment to it; to introduce them to the terms 'canon', 'accompaniment' and 'ostinato'.

Resources

Cassette: side 1, activity 16

Chime bars G and D
Copymaster 11

Presentation
Teach the children the melody and words of the following hymn.

Starting note: G
Count in: 1 2 1

Glory to thee my God

Glory to Thee my God this night
For all the blessings of the light
Keep me, oh keep me king of kings
Beneath Thine own almighty wings.

When the children are confident in singing the words, add the two-note accompaniment as indicated on the copymaster. After a while, this task could be handed over to one of the children. Next, divide the class into two groups. Group I starts to sing on its own. Group II then starts the song when the first group sings the word 'my' (marked with an asterisk on the music and copymaster).

Remember to ask the children to listen very carefully to each other and to the underlying accompaniment so that they keep together and do not drown each other out. This should be a harmonious performance, not a race to the finish first or a competition to hear who can sing loudest.

When the class is able to sing the canon in two groups, divide them into three groups. The third group will start singing when group two is singing the word indicated by the asterisk.

Discussion
Explain to the children that when several groups sing the same tune one after another in this way, they are said to be singing 'a round', or to be singing in *canon*. When an instrumental part is played as the singers perform, this is known as an *accompaniment*, and when the accompaniment revolves around the same notes in a constant pattern as happens here, the accompaniment is said to be an *ostinato* accompaniment.

Draw the children's attention to the fact that, in this tune, all the notes are the same length.

Background information
The tunes to many of the hymns sung today are very old. This canon is over 400 years old and was written by Thomas Tallis, who lived in the time of Henry VIII. As a young man, Thomas Tallis worked in a monastery as an organist and as a composer of music for the services. But then the king decided to close down the monasteries. He sold the rich treasures, paintings and books in them and, in many cases, gave the lands and buildings to his friends who made them into large mansions for themselves. Others were simply allowed to fall into ruin. Because of this Tallis had to leave his job at the monastery, but eventually he went to work for the king himself as organist at the royal chapel. During his lifetime he wrote a large amount of music; this canon is one of his most famous pieces. It is sung as a canon or round in three groups, but one of his other pieces was written for 40 groups!

Listening
Play the children a recording of the 40-part piece mentioned above – the motet 'Spem in Alium'.

Draw their attention to the way that the music seems to flow on without a break, because as one part finishes another one starts. Compare this with the effect of the canon which can also appear to be going on without a break, especially if it is sung through two or three times by each group.

Glo-ry to Thee my God this night For all the ble-ssings of the light. Keep

me, oh keep me King of kings Be-neath Thine own al-migh-ty wings.

17. MAKE UP YOUR OWN CANON

Purpose
To enable the children to improvise their own canons.

Resources
Chime bars C D E G A

Presentation
Ask one child to improvise a short tune based on those notes. Each note should be of the same length, as in the Tallis canon. Help the child to refine the tune and to remember it. When the child has done so, help him or

her to teach it to a second child. Both children should then practise playing the made up tune several times together. When they are both thoroughly confident about doing so, ask the first child to start. Then ask the second child to start a little later. Both should play the same tune twice. Because of the limited number of notes used and the nature of the notes selected, the result will be a canon, whatever the point at which the second child starts to play.

When the children have mastered this, encourage them to listen to what they are producing and, through experimentation and discussion, refine it so that it is a pleasing piece of music for others to listen to.

Further performance opportunities
When the pupils have gained sufficient confidence in the performance of the Tallis canon, or their own composition, encourage them to present the performance to their classmates or to other children in the school. This could be an element in assembly, for example.

18. STAMPING AND CLAPPING SONG

Purpose
To give the children further experience of marking the underlying beat of a song with a variety of movements; to enable them to reproduce a number of simple rhythmic patterns and to use these to create accompaniments to the song learnt; to develop their awareness of the effects of balance and volume on a performance and of the impact of various types of grouping on these elements; to enable them to experiment with various effects of instrumentation, volume and texture; to perform, record and appraise their performances.

Resources
Cassette: side 1, activity 18
Copymasters 12 and 13
Space for movement
Chime bars: B, C D G
Three groups of unpitched percussion instruments, e.g. tambours, castanets, rasps. (If these instruments are not available, substitute alternative unpitched percussion instruments. Please see pages 6–8 for the range of instruments which falls into this category).

Presentation
Using the cassette, **Copymaster 12** and the suggestions

presented in the introduction to this book, teach the children the following song.

Starting note: G
Count in: 1 2 1 2

Stamping and Clapping Song

Now we're going to dance and sing
So join hands and make a ring
Dance and sing and move around
All tread lightly on the ground.
Stamp your feet go clap! clap! clap!
Stamp your feet go clap! clap! clap!
Don't get any faster.

When they can sing the song fairly confidently, ask the children to move around the room in time to the underlying beat and/or mark the beat with the movements suggested by the words. When they can do this, ask the whole class to sing the words 'dance and sing' and to clap the rhythm for those words. Now divide the class into two groups: group 1 should sing the tune, group 2 should say and clap the rhythm of the words 'dance and sing'. They should practise saying the words increasingly softly, until eventually they are just thinking them. But do emphasise that they should continue to think them, otherwise they will soon cease to be synchronised with the rest of the performers. When they can clap the rhythmic pattern accurately, ask them to transfer the pattern onto unpitched percussion instruments.

From here you can progress to dividing the class into three groups: group 1 sings the song, group 2 plays the rhythmic pattern just learnt, and group 3 plays unpitched percussion instruments on the beat marked 1 each time.

Now help the children experiment with different types and numbers of instruments for each of the parts and to focus on the way that balance can be produced in a performance. Ask them questions such as the following:

● What is the effect of having one as opposed to several instruments playing a part?
● Is it better to have several performers playing softly or to reduce the number of performers?

- How can they avoid drowning the sound of the singers? (They could ask the singers to sing more loudly or they could ask the instrumentalists to play more softly.)

Now concentrate on the effects of different types of instruments on the performance. Do the children think that some instruments are more suitable than others? Why do they think this? Should the instruments or numbers of performers be altered from one verse to another to suit the character of the words?

Remember that there are no right or wrong answers here. The important thing is that the children should be given the opportunity to experiment, to listen, to discuss and to explain their preferences and to refine their performances. As they do so, they will begin to realise that, within any performance, there are endless possibilities.

From here you can progress to adding the chime bar accompaniment to the song. Here again involve the children in discussing and experimenting with various effects of volume and balance.

When they have discussed and experimented with various effects, decide on one version and practise this. This could then be performed to a class from elsewhere in the school or it could be recorded on tape and played back to the performers for their comments.

Use the performance evaluation sheet (**Copymaster 13**) to help the children make notes on the various effects to which they are listening and to evaluate the impact of the final performance. You could also use that copymaster at other points in your lessons during the key stage to give your pupils more practice in relation to listening and appraising.

Now we're going to dance and sing. So join hands and
Dance and sing and move a - round. All tread light - ly

make a ring. Stamp your feet go clap! clap! clap!
on the ground.

Stamp your feet go clap! clap! clap! Don't get a - ny fas - ter.

19. FROM VERY SOFT TO VERY LOUD

Purpose
To introduce the children to the Italian terms and signs used to indicate gradations of volume; to give them experience of reacting to such terminology when involved in group improvisations and to apply the terminology to listening activities; to involve the children in directing and responding to direction.

Resources
Copymasters 14 and 15
A range of instruments, one for each member of the class or group involved.

Presentation
Explain to the children that, in music, we often use Italian words to indicate how it ought to be performed. Italian words are used because, for a long time, the Italians were the leading performers and composers in Europe. Tell them that in order to show that music should be LOUD we use the term FORTE or the

abbreviation 'f'; to show that it should be SOFT we use the term PIANO, which is abbreviated to 'p'. Explain that the full name for the piano is 'pianoforte', i.e. an instrument which can be played both softly and loudly. Before the invention of this instrument it was not possible to play softly and loudly by using different pressure on the same keys. Then explain that, for VERY LOUD, we use the term FORTISSIMO (sign: 'ff') and for VERY SOFT, we use PIANISSIMO, abbreviated to 'pp'.

Draw their attention to the signs on **Copymaster 14**. Cut out these signs and mount them on separate cards. Then attach a plywood handle to each one, so that they can be held up easily for others to see. Now you are ready to perform a group improvisation. You could do this with the whole class or with groups of children at various times.

Give each child in the group an instrument. Ask one of them to act as 'conductor'. The conductor is given the four signs which you have prepared. As the sign is displayed by the conductor, the performers react appropriately by altering the volume. Give them the opportunity to get used to reacting to the signs. Then begin to refine the performances. This can be done in a variety of ways. For example, you could divide the

performers into 3 groups: with group 1 playing wooden instruments, group 2 playing skin instruments and group 3 playing metal instruments. The performance could start with the wooden instruments playing pianissimo, followed by the skin instruments also playing pianissimo. The metal instruments could then play loudly. This could be followed by groups 1 and 2 playing piano. Then all the instruments could play fortissimo.

You could develop this idea further by asking two groups to play simultaneously but at differing volumes. (You would need two conductors for this or ask the one conductor to hold up two signs simultaneously.) Changing the indications round for the two groups would produce interesting effects in terms of balance.

There are obviously endless possibilities. The important thing is to encourage the children to reflect on the effects of the differences in volume and to encourage them to use the contrasts to give shape to their improvisation. When they find effects they particularly like, they should be encouraged to refine and develop them further and to practise reproducing the desired effects. They could then record these using **Copymaster 15**.

20. RHYTHM GAMES

Purpose
To give the children further practice in reproducing rhythmic patterns; to enable them to perform several patterns simultaneously and then to transfer these to instruments.

Resources
Range of unpitched percussion instruments
Copymaster 16
Tambour for the teacher
Cassette: side 1, activity 20

Presentation
Arrange the children so that they are sitting in a circle. Ask them what their favourite food is. They might say 'fish and chips'. Ask them to say this in time with a beat as follows:

				Fish and	Chips
1	2	1	2	1	2

Another might say 'Curry'. Again ask that child to say the word to a beat as follows:

				Curry	
1	2	1	2	1	2

Go on round the circle. The rhythms of some words are shown on the copymaster.

When this has been done, ask all the children to tap out a regular beat on their laps. Then, as you point to them, ask the children in turn to say their favourite food several times before you move onto the next person.

From here you can progress to a modification of

approach. Start the activity in the same way, but this time, instead of stopping when you point to the next person, each child should continue to say and clap out his/her own rhythm. Eventually a whole range of rhythms will be playing together.

Remind the children that they must continue to say the words for their foods as they clap, otherwise they will not clap accurately. But urge them not to say the words too loudly and to listen to the others in the group. You might find it helpful to tap out the beat on the tambour, to make sure that they keep together.

When they can do this confidently, ask them to think the words in their heads and to clap as before.

You will need to return to this activity several times to help the children consolidate their skills. To maintain interest, change the stimulus so that they are not always clapping out the rhythms of food names. You could use the names of football teams, their own names, towns on a map, countries which they might have visited on holiday, and so on.

When the children have had sufficient practice at this type of activity, ask them to transfer their clapping to instruments, starting with unpitched instruments.

As with other improvisation activities in this book, encourage the children to listen very carefully to the effects being created and to help you to refine them and give them shape. Thus you might choose to start with one instrument, build up to a point where the whole group is playing and then return gradually to one instrument. Alternatively, you could start with lots of instruments playing, then have a few performers and end with all instruments playing together again. Obviously the possibilities are endless.

Extension

From here you could progress to using pitched instruments. If you do so, ask the children to use the following five notes only on each instrument:

C   D   E   G   A

The use of this series of notes (known as a pentatonic scale) ensures a pleasing blend of sounds.

As with the previous activities make sure that the children listen very carefully to the overall effect and that, through listening, discussion and experimentation, they are helped to refine it. Again, remember that this activity will take time and you will need to return to it from time to time and intersperse parts of it into the other activities included in this book.

21. HOW LOUD OR SOFT IS IT?

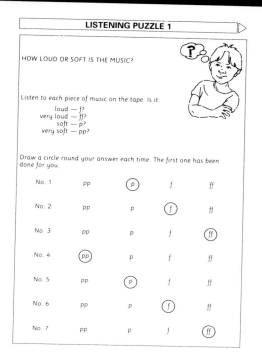

LISTENING PUZZLE 1

HOW LOUD OR SOFT IS THE MUSIC?

Listen to each piece of music on the tape. Is it:

loud — f?
very loud — ff?
soft — p?
very soft — pp?

Draw a circle round your answer each time. The first one has been done for you.

No. 1	pp	ⓟ	f	ff
No. 2	pp	p	ⓕ	ff
No. 3	pp	p	f	ⓕⓕ
No. 4	ⓟⓟ	p	f	ff
No. 5	pp	ⓟ	f	ff
No. 6	pp	p	ⓕ	ff
No. 7	pp	p	f	ⓕⓕ

Purpose

To give the children practice in identifying whether pieces of music which they hear are loud, very loud, soft or very soft.

Resources

Cassette: side 1, activity 21
Copymaster 17

Presentation

Play the children all the musical extracts on the cassette side x, track y, one after the other. This is important because the loudness of a piece of music is relative. Therefore the children will need to be able to hear each extract in relation to the others. Then play each extract one at a time – more than once if necessary – and ask the children to circle their answers on **Copymaster 17**.

22. THE WINDMILL

Purpose

To give the children further experience of moving in time to the beat of a song and of adding an accompaniment to it; to enable them to identify and react through movement to changes of tempo and to stepwise melodic progression.

Resources

Cassette: side 1, activity 22
Chime bars arranged into two sets:
    Set 1: D A
    Set 2: E F#G
Copymasters 18 and 19
Space for movement

Presentation

Using the cassette, **Copymaster 18** and the suggestions made at the beginning of the book, teach the children the following song.

Starting note: D
Count in: 1 2 1 2

The Windmill Song

1. See that windmill on the hill?
   Watch the sails they're never still
   Never still from morn till night
   Grinding corn with all their might

2. When the sun begins to shine
   And the weather's warm and fine
   Then the wind begins to fall
   And the sails they start to stall

3. When the wind blows strong again
   And the gusts ride o'er the fen
   Then the sails begin to glide
   Faster, faster on they ride

In performing this song, aim to produce a smooth melodic flow. When the children can perform it with a fair degree of confidence and accuracy, draw their attention to the way that the tune moves. In the first line, it moves upwards by steps, finishing with a slight move down by step at the end. This pattern is repeated in the second line. In line three, the melody jumps about a bit. Then, in the last line, it moves in steps again, this time in a downwards direction. Help the children to appreciate this by asking them to make smooth rising movements with their hands when singing each of the first two lines and then a smooth downwards movement in the last line.

When they have done this, ask them to find spaces for themselves around the room where they can move without bumping into each other. Now ask them to experiment with finding movements which reflect the movements of a windmill. They could move their arms in an arc in front of them. They could step round in a circle on the spot. They could link arms with other children and move in a circle. When they have experimented with movements and produced a wide range of them, ask the children to sing the song again and to make their movements in time to the beat of the music.

Now discuss with the children how a windmill works. When it is not being used, its sails are anchored. When it starts, it takes a little time for it to build up speed and to move at a regular pace. Also, when the wind drops, its speed is affected. Play them the second and third verses of the song on tape so that they can hear the effect of the changes of tempo. Then ask them to perform it in this way.

Explain to the children that the term we use in music for getting faster is ACCELERANDO. It is a very similar word to ACCELERATE which we use when describing cars getting faster. The words for getting slower, on the other hand, are RITARDANDO or RALLENTANDO (for simplicity we will be using 'Rallentando' throughout these activities). Let them read these on **Copymaster 19**.

From here, you can move to adding the first chime bar accompaniment to the song. When this is being performed confidently, add the second part to the accompaniment. Here the player will need to know exactly on which words to play. To make sure that the accompaniment is in time, the player should sing along with the rest and then add the accompaniment at the appropriate time.

Extension

Play the children the musical extracts on cassette side 1, activity 22 and ask them to decide whether they get faster or get slower. When they have decided, they should complete **Copymaster 19**. The correct answers are given below.

GETTING FASTER AND GETTING SLOWER

We show that music gets faster by using the word ACCELERANDO or the sign ACCEL.

We show that music gets slower by using the word RALLENTANDO or the sign RALL.

LISTENING PUZZLE

Listen to each piece of music on the tape. Does it get faster or does it get slower? Draw a circle round your answer each time. The first one has been done for you.

1. ACCELERANDO	(RALLENTANDO)
2. RALL.	(ACCEL.)
3. (RALL.)	ACCEL.
4. RALL.	(ACCEL.)
5. (ACCEL.)	RALL.
6. (RALL.)	ACCEL.

See— that— wind - mill on the hill? Watch— the— sails they're ne - ver

still. Ne - ver still from morn till night. Grin - ding corn with all their might.

23. INSTRUMENTAL SQUARES

Purpose
To give the children further experience of performing rhythmic patterns as a group and applying rhythmic squares in making up their own patterns for performance and in notating rhythmic patterns they have heard.

Resources
Copymaster 20
Cassette: side 1, activity 23
Triangles
Drums
Claves
Tambourines

Presentation
On the copymaster, you will see a series of four rhythmic patterns: one line per instrument. Listen to each one being performed on the cassette. Ask the children to clap each line and to follow it on the copymaster. Now

ask the triangle players to transfer the first pattern on to their instruments; the drummers to transfer the second pattern to their instruments and so on. When each group can perform its line accurately, ask them all to play together. To do so, you will need to keep a regular beat by beating your foot or by using the metronome. Do not forget to count them in so that they all know when to start.

Extension
When the above activity has been successfully completed, make several copies of **Copymaster 20**, mount them onto cards and cut them into squares. The children can now rearrange these for performance by each other. Because of the increased number of cards, the extracts can be considerably extended.

In addition to creating patterns for performance, the children could also play very simple patterns to each other, which they then have to notate, using the cards.

24. JOGGIN' SONG

Purpose
To give the children further experience of adding a simple pitched percussion accompaniment to a song that they have learnt and of performing successive verses of it at different speeds; to give them the opportunity to reflect on the effectiveness of their own and each other's performances.

Resources
Cassette: side 1, activity 24
Chime bars: D G and A
Tape recorder
Copymaster 21

Presentation
Start by teaching the children the following song:

Starting note: G
Count in: 1 2 3 4 1 2 3 4

1. Joggin' up and down in my shiny new trainers
   Joggin' up and down in my shiny new trainers
   Joggin' up and down in my shiny new trainers
   All around the country.

2. Sole's come off and my left foot's hurting,
   Sole's come off and my left foot's hurting,
   Sole's come off and my left foot's hurting,
   Won't get back this morning.

3. Got my second breath and I'm running faster,
   Got my second breath and I'm running faster,
   Got my second breath and I'm running faster,
   Might get back this evening.

4. Both feet are sore and I am puffing,
   Both feet are sore and I am puffing,
   Both feet are sore and I am puffing,
   I'll go by car tomorrow!

When the children can sing it fairly confidently, try adding the accompaniment on the chime bars as shown on the copymaster. Start by adding it yourself and then inviting individual children to play it. As in previous activities, make sure that two beaters are used: the left-hand beater for the note D and the right-hand beater for the other two notes.

In addition to the pitched percussion, focus on the unpitched percussion. Start by clapping out the rhythm of the words: 'Shiny new trainers'. Then transfer this to an unpitched percussion instrument. As in other pieces of this type, resist the temptation to ask too many children to perform it at the same time. To ensure involvement, it is better to arrange for the children to take turns in performing accompaniments, otherwise the balance and musical quality of the performance is impaired.

When this is being performed fairly accurately, draw attention to the words of the second verse. These suggest that the speed (tempo) should be slower. Practise singing it at a slower speed and then adding the accompaniment once more. To ensure that everybody keeps together, start by counting out the beat at a slower tempo and then indicating the slower beat by moving your hand or foot or head in time to it. Encourage the children to keep in time with this slower speed. When the slower speed has been successfully

established and the children can sing the first two verses, turn your attention to the third and fourth verses. These suggest further changes in tempo: a speeding up in verse three and a slowing down in verse 4. This last verse should be even slower than the second verse. When this has been practised, sing the whole song through without any breaks.

Encourage the children to reflect and comment on the quality of the performance and the success or otherwise of the effect that you are trying to achieve. You could do this in several ways, e.g. by recording the performance, playing it back and inviting comments or asking one or two children to act as an audience and to present their verdict on the effectiveness of the performance.

Jo - ggin' up and down in my shi - ny new trai - ners

Jo - ggin' up and down in my shi - ny new trai - ners Jo - ggin' up and down in my

shi - ny new trai - ners All a - round the coun - try.

25. CAN YOU HEAR THE DIFFERENT SPEEDS?

Purpose
To introduce the children to the Italian terms used to denote varying speeds (tempi) in music and to give them practise in applying these terms when describing the tempi of musical extracts played to them. (NB tempo = speed, tempi = speeds.)

Resources
Cassette: side 2, activity 25
Copymaster 22

Presentation
Remind the children of the changes of speeds which they heard and performed in Activity 22. Explain to them that in music we often use the following Italian words to show how slowly or quickly a piece should be performed. One word for SLOW is LARGO, and one word for FAST is ALLEGRO. When the children have learnt and can remember these terms, play them the extracts on the cassette and ask them to complete the copymaster. The answers are as follows: No. 1 = Allegro, No. 2 = Largo, No. 3 = Largo, No. 4 = Allegro, No. 5 = Allegro, No. 6 = Largo.

26. IN HOW MANY WAYS CAN YOU MAKE A SOUND?

Purpose

To help the children explore given instruments and discover a variety of ways of producing sounds on them, in order to extend the range of sounds available for improvisation and composition activities.

Resources

Cassette: side 2, activity 26
An unpitched instrument, e.g. the tambourine.
Copymaster 23

Presentation

Arrange the children in a circle and teach them the following song:

Starting note: D
Count in: 1 2 3 4, 1 2 3 (NB In this song the first word starts on the 4th beat of the bar not the first beat as has often been the case in other songs encountered so far in this book.)

In How Many Ways?

In how many ways can you make a sound
As you pass this instrument round and round?
Make sure that the sound you make is new
We want lots of sounds and not just a few.

When the children can perform the song fairly confidently, draw their attention to the tambourine in your hand. Tell them that, as they sing, they should pass this instrument round the circle. When the music stops, the person holding the instrument should make a sound on it. The song will then restart and the instrument will again be passed round in time to the music. When the music next stops, the person holding it should produce a sound which is entirely different from the one already produced by the previous performer.

The game continues in this way. Any child who produces a sound which has already been produced is out. The game finishes when everybody is out.

When the game has finished, use the copymaster to list the sounds which they made, how they were produced and to find a word to describe each sound. The sounds of the tambourine for example might be described as follows:

INSTRUMENT	HOW DID YOU PLAY IT?	WHAT SOUND DID IT MAKE?
Tambourine	*Shaking*	*Jingly*
Tambourine	*Rubbing hands on skin of instrument*	*Swishy*
Tambourine	*Hitting the wooden part*	*Hollow*

This could be the basis of a classroom display under a title such as SOUND EXPERIMENTS. You can return to this game several times, using different instruments. You could occasionally return to instruments already featured to see whether the possibilities can be extended further. With some classes, you might have to prepare and prompt them by asking them to think of three different sounds they might produce on the instrument, before actually starting the game.

When you have worked on unpitched instruments, extend the activity to include pitched percussion instruments. If, at later stages, you feel that pupils are not making a sufficiently varied use of sounds in their compositions, you could always return to this as an introductory or supplementary activity to the composition work.

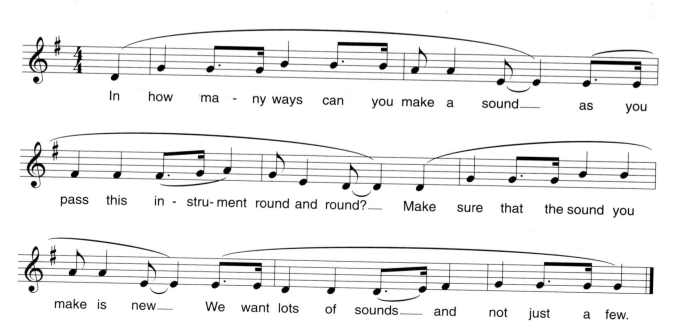

In how ma-ny ways can you make a sound___ as you pass this in-stru-ment round and round?___ Make sure that the sound you make is new___ We want lots of sounds___ and not just a few.

39

27. CHANGING SPEEDS

Purpose
To give the children practice in exploring a range of speeds and volumes when improvising and in conducting or responding to a conductor.

Resources
Copymasters 24 and 14
Instrument for each member of the class or group

Presentation
Make copies of **Copymaster 24**, mount them onto cards, cut them out and attach a stiff card or plywood handle to each one. Give each child in the group an instrument and arrange them so that they are all facing one child who acts as the conductor. Group the instrumentalists in a variety of ways, e.g. all wooden instruments together, all ringing instruments together, etc., reminding them of the work done on tempo changes in Activity 22.

Now the children should begin to play when directed to do so by the conductor. Until the children have got the idea, it might be best if you act as the conductor. This role can later be taken by the children in turn. Since this is the type of activity to which you can return on several occasions, there will be plenty of opportunities for the children to have the experience of directing a performance.

Depending on the card which the conductor holds up, the instrumentalists should play slowly or quickly or alter their speed appropriately. After an initial run-through to ensure that the children are responding correctly to the speed indications, encourage them to give shape to their improvisations. As with earlier activities of this type, the possibilities are endless. Two possible shapes that you might wish to use as a starting point are given below. Remember that these are just starting points and are not definitive.

Shape 1
Group 1: Largo
All Players: Largo
Group 2: Allegro
All Players: Allegro
Group 3: Start Allegro. Then Rallentando to Largo
Final short 'chord' from all players.

Shape 2
Group 1 players start Largo. They continue playing as Group 2 enters.
After a few moments, both groups Accelerando until they are all playing Allegro.
As the first groups reach Allegro, Group 3 enters.
A few moments later Group 1 stops playing, followed by Group 2.
Group 3 continues on its own but then, after a few moments, they get slower until they play Largo.
The piece finishes with all performers playing their first idea now Largo

As in earlier activities of this type, it is very important to give the children the opportunity to experiment with various effects and to discuss and refine their ideas.

Extension
The improvisation activity described above could be extended by asking the children to respond to two types of indications: those for tempo (**Copymaster 24**) and also for volume (**Copymaster 14**). An even greater variety of patterns can be produced in this way. It has been claimed that children do not have full mastery of a concept until they can combine it with other concepts. This activity allows for such development.

28. WAKE UP! WAKE UP!

Purpose
To teach the children to sing a simple song which can be performed as a canon in two parts; to enable them to add simple chordal accompaniments to the song and to listen for balance of volume as they perform in groups and as a whole ensemble.

Resources
Cassette: side 2, activity 28
Chime bars arranged into two sets:
    Set 1: Bb D F
    Set 2: F A ℃
Copymaster 25

Presentation
Using the cassette, **Copymaster 25** and the suggestions found in the introduction, teach the children to sing the song. Aim for a bright, cheerful sound in the perfor-

mance, making sure that there is an accent on the words on beats marked 1 (see **Copymaster 25**).

Starting note: Bb
Count in: 1 2 3 1 2 (NB The first note of the vocal part starts on beat 3)

Wake Up!

Wake up! Wake up! It is the dawn
The sun's shining brightly to ripen the corn

Now add the accompaniment. To do so, ask two groups of children to play the chime bars already set out. Group 1 will play the first set of chime bars while group 2 will play the second set.

The pattern for the accompaniment is as follows, with a chord being played on the first beat of every bar:

Group 1   Group 1   Group 2   Group 1

This is played as an introduction and twice more while the singers are performing. As before, make sure that the instrumentalists also sing, so that they can keep time with their fellow performers.

The next stage is to practise singing the song as a canon. Divide the class into two groups of approximately equal numbers. Impress on them that the purpose of the activity is to produce a balanced sound and that this is not a competition to hear which group can sing the louder. The second group should enter when the first group has reached the point indicated by the asterisk (*). When this has been practised with voices only, add the accompaniment. As before, play an introduction before the first group enters. Because the second group enters later, the accompanists will have to play their pattern one time more than previously. When the second group has

finished singing, the accompanists should keep playing for yet another one time through their pattern to provide what is termed a 'postlude' or conclusion by musicians. Therefore, the overall pattern for the accompanists will be as follows:

Introduction:	Group 1	Group 1	Group 2	Group 1
First vocal part performing:	Group 1	Group 1	Group 2	Group 1
Second vocal part performing:	Group 1	Group 1	Group 2	Group 1
Second vocal part continuing:	Group 1	Group 1	Group 2	Group 1
Postlude:	Group 1	Group 1	Group 2	Group 1

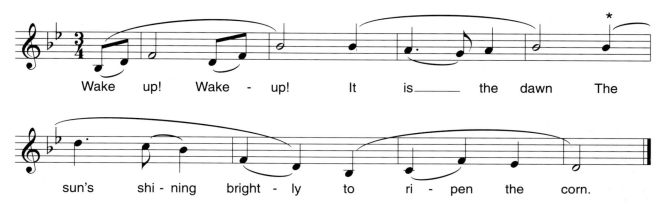

29. THE ORCHESTRA SONG

Purpose
To extend the children's understanding of how musical sounds are produced; to enable them to differentiate between sounds which are bowed, plucked, banged, scraped, shaken or plucked; to give them further experience of marking the beat of a song through movement; to enable them to sing a song involving several parts.

Resources
Cassette: side 2, activity 29
Copymasters 26 and 27

Presentation
With the aid of the cassette, **Copymaster 26** and the suggestions in the introduction, teach the children the following song. Start by asking the whole class to sing each verse.

Starting note: D
Count in: 1 2 1 2 (NB The first note starts on the second half of the second beat)

The Orchestra Song

1. I play upon the violin
   I draw my bow along
   The sound I make is sweet and smooth
   To suit this merry song

   Chorus: La la la la la
             La la la la la
             La la la la la
             La la la la la

2. I blow upon my trumpet
   Ta ran tan ta tarra ta
   I wake up all both far and near
   Ta ran tan ta tarra ta

   Chorus: Tarra ta tarra ta
             Tarra ran ta ta
             Tarra ta tarra ta
             Tarra ran ta ta

3. I beat upon my drum
   And make a great big clashing sound
   They hear my drum and cymbal
   For many miles around

Chorus: Boom boom boom boom
Boom clash clash boom
Boom boom boom boom
Boom clash clash boom

4. I can play pizzicato
I pluck and make short sounds
I tiptoe up I tip toe down
I tip toe all around

Chorus: Pluck pluck
Pluck pluck pluck
Pluck pluck
Pluck pluck pluck

5. I shake and tap the tambourine
And clap the castanet
I think these are the best sounds
That you'll have heard as yet

Chorus: Shake shake shake shake
Shake clap clap shake
Shake shake shake shake
Shake clap clap shake

When the children are able to sing the words and the tune fairly confidently, invite them to march round the room in time to the beat of the music and make appropriate gestures to represent the instruments which are mentioned in each verse.

Discuss with the children the way that sounds are produced on the various instruments that have been mentioned. Listen to the taped examples of these instruments, in order to familiarise them further with these sounds.

In order to help focus the children's attention further, you could produce a classroom display headed INSTRUMENTS WE HAVE HEARD. The children could then enter the names of instruments which they have encountered in radio or television broadcasts or at other points in the day. They could record who heard what, with the date each time. From here you can progress to asking the children to listen to the listening puzzle on the cassette and to complete **Copymaster 27**.

Extension

When the children can sing each verse separately, divide them into groups, one for each instrument. Then sing the song in the following order so that, with each successive verse, more and more parts will be heard in the chorus.

Verse 1: Group 1 sings verse and chorus 1
Verse 2: Group 2 sings verse and chorus 2. As the chorus is sung, group 1 sings chorus 1 at the same time.

LISTENING PUZZLE 4

WHICH INSTRUMENT CAN YOU HEAR?

On the tape, you will hear six instruments being played one after the other. Listen very carefully and draw a ring round the name of the instrument which you think is playing. The first one has been done for you.

1. Violin	Trumpet	(Triangle)	Tambourine
2. (Trumpet)	Drum	Cymbal	Violin
3. Castanets	(Cymbal)	Trumpet	Violin
4. Drum	Trumpet	Recorder	(Chime bars)
5. (Violin)	Trumpet	Drum	Triangle
6. Trumpet	(Drum)	Cymbal	Recorder

Verse 3: Group 3 sings verse and chorus 3. As the chorus is sung, group 1 sings chorus 1, group 2 sings chorus 2.
Verse 4: Group 4 sings verse and chorus 4. As the chorus is sung, group 1 sings chorus 1, group 2 sings chorus 2 and group 3 sings chorus 3.
Verse 5: Group 5 sings verse and chorus 5. As the chorus is sung, group 1 sings chorus 1, group 2 sings chorus 2, group 3 sings chorus 3, group 4 sings chorus 4.

In this way the texture will build up. As with the work on canons, encourage the children to listen to each other and do not let them shout each other down.

Do not be surprised if some of the children find this extension activity difficult. You might well need to return to it at a later point, when they have had more experience of singing canons. On the other hand, even if the whole class cannot perform it, there might be a small group who could do so. As with any subject, it is important to ensure that you cater for a wide range of abilities within your class and present the children with appropriate challenges.

30. GO TELL AUNT NANCY

Purpose
To give the children further experience of identifying groupings of one-beat and half-beat notes in a song of performing rhythmic combinations, based on these groupings; and of converting sounds into signs and signs into sounds.

Resources
Copymasters 28 and 29
Cassette: side 2, activity 30
Chime bars arranged into 2 sets:
    Set 1: F A C'
    Set 2: C E G
(NB C' in the first group should be at a higher pitch than the C in group 2)
Space for movement

Presentation
With the aid of the cassette, **Copymaster 28** and the advice included in the introduction to the book, teach the children the following song:

Starting note: A
Count in: 12 12

Go Tell Aunt Nancy

1. Go tell Aunt Nancy
    Go tell Aunt Nancy
    Go tell Aunt Nancy
    The old grey goose is dead.

2. The one that she's been saving
    The one that she's been saving
    The one that she's been saving
    To make a feather bed.

3. She died in the mill pond
    She died in the mill pond
    She died in the mill pond
    Standing on her head.

4. The goslings are crying
    The goslings are crying
    The goslings are crying
    Because their mum is dead.

When the children are able to perform the song confidently and accurately, ask them to tap the beat gently on their laps as they sing. Then ask them to clap the *rhythm* of the music, i.e. by clapping on each syllable as it is sung. When they are able to do this, divide the class into two groups. All the children should sing but group 1 should tap out the beat as they do so, while group 2 claps out the rhythm.

Now, using **Copymaster 29**, ask the children to march on the spot as they sing the song. In doing so, they will be marking the beat as they sing. The next stage is to ask them to clap the rhythm as they march on the spot. In some instances, you might find it better to divide the class in two, with one half marching on the spot to the beat, while the other half claps out the rhythms of the words. Ring the changes in such an arrangement so that all the children have the opportunity to perform both activities. Also make sure that, regardless of whether they are marking the beat or the rhythm, all the children are singing. Unless they do so, the synchronisation will be lost. Furthermore, they will not be feeling the effects of the rhythm and the beat as they combine.

Focus on the fact that some beats have one syllable or sound on them, while others have two. For example, in the first line, there is one syllable per beat on 'Go', 'Nan' and 'cy' but two syllables on 'tell Aunt'. Point this out to the children.

Now ask them to focus on the last two lines. In the penultimate line, there is one sound to the beat on: 'Go', 'Nan' and 'dead' but two sounds per beat on: 'tell Aunt', 'cy the', 'old grey' and 'goose is'. Explain to the class that one sound per beat = da, and two sounds per beat = di-di. Using this system, they should be able to tell you that the first line runs as follows:

da di-di da da

Now work on the other lines of the song in the same way. Ask the children to write the syllables over the feet marked on the copymaster. In this way, they should be able to build up the following picture:

Go tell Aunt Nancy Go tell Aunt Nan- cy
da di- di   da da da di- di   da   da
Go tell Aunt Nancy the old grey goose is dead
da di- di   da di-di di- di   di - di da

Again remember that there are several activities in this section. Don't expect to be able to cover them all in one lesson. You might consider pursuing part of the activity with small groups rather than tackling it all as a full class activity. This is a decision which you must make in light of your own confidence, the circumstances in which you are working and the size, experience, interests and abilities of your class.

44

Extension
Ask the children:

- to listen to the rhythms of the words;

- to clap them out;
- to clap them out and also to maintain the beat by marching on the spot.

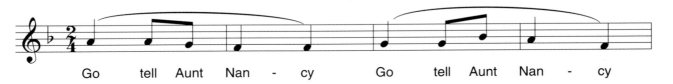

Go   tell   Aunt   Nan - cy   Go   tell   Aunt   Nan - cy

Go   tell   Aunt   Nan - cy   the   old   grey   goose   is   dead.

31. 'CELTIC' LAMENT

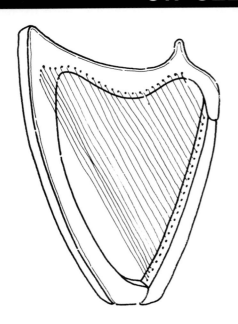

Starting note: E
Count in: 1 2 3 1 2

Celtic Lament

The dawn is breaking over the sea
Its warmth is washing over the lea
Alas my heart will never be free
Till my dear loved one returns home to me.

When the children can sing the song fairly confidently, concentrate on ensuring that each line is sung in one breath and that the effect of the singing is relaxed and gentle. (The section on breathing on page 5 of the introduction will be a useful reference for you here.) Also make sure that, when the children do breathe, they do so very softly, so as not to break across the mood of the song.

When they have mastered this, ask them to stand with their arms stretched out in front of them. As the music rises in pitch, ask them to raise their arms accordingly. As it goes down in pitch, ask them to lower their arms so that they are describing the shape of the melody with their movements. Draw their attention to the fact that the music is smooth because each movement of the pitch is from one note to the next. This melody is therefore described as 'moving by step'.

Play the track again. This time, ask the children to listen very carefully to the instrument being used as an accompaniment. This instrument is the harp. There are several types of harp, but this particular one is known as an Irish or Celtic harp. Listen to other examples of harp music.

Purpose
To help the children identify melodic patterns which move by step; to give them greater experience of listening to the sounds of the harp.

Resources
Space for movement
Cassette: side 2, activity 31
Copymaster 30

Presentation
Using the cassette, **Copymaster 30** and the ideas presented in the introduction, teach the children the following song.

The dawn— is brea - king o - ver the sea. Its warmth— is

wa - shing o - ver the lea A - las— my heart— will

ne - ver be free Till my— dear loved one re - turns home to me.

32. JOHN SMITH FELLOW FINE

Purpose
To give the children further practice in identifying groupings of one-beat and half-beat notes in a song; to enable them to read and perform further rhythmic combinations, based on these groupings; to identify rhythm combinations through listening and be able to notate rhythmic patterns.

Resources
Cassette: side 2, activity 32
Copymasters 31–33
Space for movement

Presentation
With the aid of the cassette, **Copymaster 31** and the

advice given in the introduction, teach the following song to the children.

Starting note: C
Count in: 1 2 1 2

John Smith

John Smith fellow fine
Can you shoe this horse of mine?
Yes sir that I can
Just as well as any man.
There's a nail upon the toe
The pony then will want to go
There's a nail upon the heel
To make the pony gallop well.
John Smith fellow fine
Can you shoe this horse of mine?
Yes sir that I can
Just as well as any man.

When they are able to perform it confidently and accurately, ask them to tap the beat gently on their laps as they sing. Next ask them to clap the rhythm of the music, i.e. by clapping on each syllable as it is sung. When they are able to do this, divide the class into two groups. All the children should sing but group 1 should tap out the beat as they do so, while group 2 claps out the rhythm. When they are able to do this accurately ask the children to march on the spot as they sing the song. In doing so, they will be marking the beat as they sing.

Now remind them of the work already done in Activity 30 (Go Tell Aunt Nancy) on one-beat and half-beat sounds. Remind them that one sound on a beat = da, and two sounds on a beat = di-di. Ask them to sing and clap the line 'John Smith fellow fine' very slowly.

46

They should then repeat this, marching on the spot as they do so. Now ask them the following questions.

- How many sounds were there on the first beat? (one sound, therefore that must be a 'da').
- How many sounds were there on the second beat? (again one sound, therefore this must also be a 'da').
- How many sounds are there on the third beat? ('fel-low' = two sounds. Therefore this is denoted by 'di-di').
- Finally there is again one sound, 'fine' (= 'da') on the next beat.

When you have done this, ask the children to sing the song through to the syllables 'da' and 'di-di', marching on the spot as they do so, in order to reinforce the relationship between rhythm and beat.

This can be followed with the listening activity, involving the cassette track indicated above and **Copymasters 32** and **33**. The correct answers are given opposite.

Remember that there are several activities in this section. Don't expect to be able to cover them all in one lesson. Given the fact that some pupils will be able to master these ideas more quickly than others, it might be a good idea to approach this activity with groups of pupils rather than with the whole class at a time.

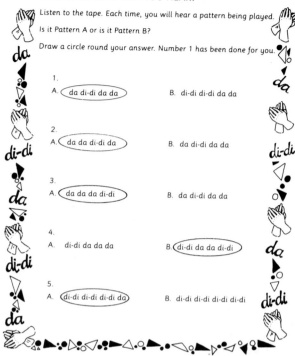

LISTENING PUZZLE 5

WHICH PATTERN CAN YOU HEAR?

Listen to the tape. Each time, you will hear a pattern being played. Is it Pattern A or is it Pattern B?

Draw a circle round your answer. Number 1 has been done for you.

1.
A. da di-di da da   B. di-di di-di da da

2.
A. da da di-di da   B. da di-di da da

3.
A. da da da di-di   B. da di-di da da

4.
A. di-di da da da   B. di-di da da da di-di

5.
A. di-di di-di di-di da   B. di-di di-di di-di di-di

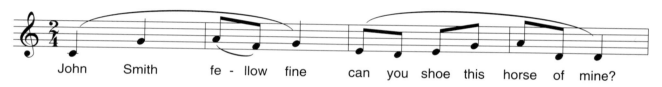

John Smith fe - llow fine can you shoe this horse of mine?

Yes sir that I can just as well as a - ny man.   *Fine*

There's a nail u - pon the toe, the po - ny then will want to go.
There's a nail u - pon the heel, to make the po - ny gal - lop well.   *D.C.*

33. MUSICAL TELEPHONES

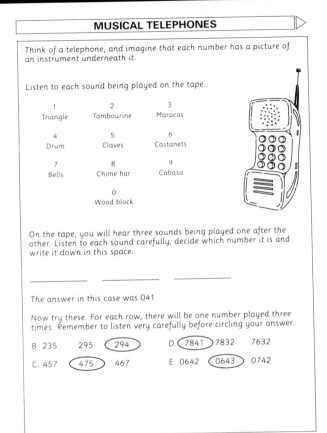

MUSICAL TELEPHONES

Think of a telephone, and imagine that each number has a picture of an instrument underneath it.

Listen to each sound being played on the tape.

1	2	3
Triangle	Tambourine	Maracas
4	5	6
Drum	Claves	Castanets
7	8	9
Bells	Chime bar	Cabasa
	0	
	Wood block	

On the tape, you will hear three sounds being played one after the other. Listen to each sound carefully, decide which number it is and write it down in this space.

_____   _____   _____

The answer in this case was 041

Now try these. For each row, there will be one number played three times. Remember to listen very carefully before circling your answer.

B. 235   295   (294)   D. (7841) 7832   7632

C. 457   (475)   467   E. 0642 (0643) 0742

Purpose

To enable the children to recognise and perform varying combinations of timbre patterns.

Resources

Cassette: side 2, activity 33
Copymasters 34 and 35
A range of pitched and unpitched percussion instruments. These should include ten different types of instrument

Presentation

Look at **Copymaster 34** with the children. Explain to them that each number on the telephone has a sound associated with it. The instrument which makes the sound is pictured beneath the numbers. They will hear nine combinations of these sounds. Each one will be played three times. They must then write a letter next to the phone number which they can hear being dialled. The answers are shown on the copymaster opposite.

Extension

Using **Copymaster 35**, ask the children to allocate one of the instruments in front of them to each of the telephone digits. Now they can make up their own telephone numbers. Do not let them make these too complicated. They should write their own numbers down on a card or a piece of paper, so that the rest of the class can see them. The children then take turns in being the caller. This is done by playing the instruments in a combination which corresponds to one of the numbers displayed by classmates. The person who has been called has to recognise his or her number and then becomes the caller. If the wrong number is called or a child does not 'lift the receiver' when his or her number 'rings' then the child responsible is out of the game.

You could return to this game several times. The children could play it as a whole class or in small groups.

34. ANOTHER WAY OF WRITING 'DA' & 'DI-DI'

Purpose
To introduce the children to another way of notating one-beat and half-beat sounds; to enable them to apply these to the reading and writing of a range of simple rhythmic patterns.

Resources
Cassette: side 2, activity 34
Copymaster 36

Presentation
Sing through the two songs 'Go Tell Aunt Nancy' and 'John Smith Fellow Fine' and remind the children of the work already done on the identification of one-beat ('da') and half-beat ('di-di') sounds in Activities 30 and 32. With the aid of **Copymaster 36**, explain to them that 'da' can be indicated with this sign: | and 'di-di' with this: ⊓. Now ask them to draw in the correct signs underneath the words on **Copymaster 36**. The correct answer can be seen on the diagram in the next column.

ANOTHER WAY TO WRITE 'DA' AND 'DI-DI'

Instead of using pictures or words you can use these signs for 'da' and 'di-di'

da = |

di-di = ⊓

Write the correct signs under the beats for 'John Smith Fellow Fine'. The first line has been done for you.

John	Smith	fel - low	fine	can you	shoe this	horse of	mine?
1	2	1	2	1	2	1	2
da	da	di - di	da	di - di	di - di	di- di	da
			⊓			⊓		⊓	⊓		

Yes	sir	that I	can	just as	well as	a - ny	man
1	2	1	2	1	2	1	2
da	da	di - di	da	di - di	di - di	di- di	da

Now do the same for 'Go Tell Aunt Nancy':

Go	tell	Aunt	Nan -	cy	Go	tell	Aunt	Nan -	cy
1	2	1		2	1	2	1		2
da	di - di	da		da	da	di - di	di - di		da

Go	tell	Aunt	Nan -	cy the old grey goose is	dead
1	2	1		2 1 2 1 2	1
da	di - di	da		di-di di - di di- di	da

Extension
You and the children can make up your own patterns and create your own performing and listening games based on the ideas presented above. As with earlier activities of this type, do not expect to be able to rush through them. You will need to return to them several times in order to give the children practice and to build up their confidence – and possibly your own. These activities might also need to be pursued with smaller groups, rather than with the whole class, in order to accommodate varying rates of progress.

35. FIND YOUR WAY ROUND THE PIANO

piano manufacturer has chosen to end the keyboard in the middle of one or other of the 2 or 3 note patterns.)

Look at one of the groups of two black notes. The white note immediately to the left of a group of this type is called C.

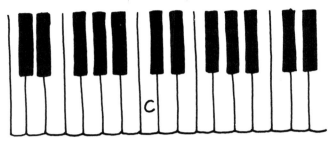

Moving to the right the white notes are called D E F G A B. Then the pattern starts again.

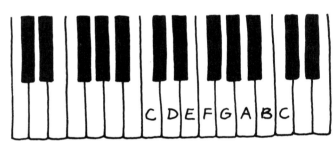

The C which is nearest the middle point of the piano is called Middle C.

When you have digested this information and are confident about it, present it to the children, using **Copymaster 39** to help you. You will probably find this easier to do with small groups of children at a time. You could then play a game of asking the children to find all the Cs on the piano, all the Fs and so on, so that they and you build up familiarity with the keyboard.

The next stage is to make copies of **Copymasters 37** and **38**. Mount them on card, cut them out and join them together to create a continuous chart. Make sure that you arrange them in the correct order.

Now find Middle C (the one nearest the centre of the instrument) and slide your chart behind the keys so that the name 'Middle C' on the chart is immediately over the Middle C key on the piano. To keep the chart in position, attach it with Bluetack to the piano lid.

Now, with the aid of **Copymaster 40**, help the children to find the notes indicated. This is an activity that can be pursued by individuals, pairs or small groups at odd times during the day and returned to at various times. Keeping the chart in place permanently on the piano will help with this.

Purpose
To introduce the children to the positioning of notes on the piano or keyboard.

Resources
A piano
Copymasters 37–40
Blutack®

Presentation
Look at the pattern of keys on the piano. They look like this.

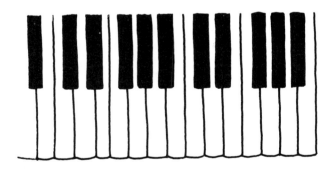

You will notice that there are more white notes than black ones. The black notes are arranged into regular patterns: 2 3 2 3 etc. (At the extreme ends you might find single black notes, but that is only because the

36. THE RAIN SONG

The Rain

The rain is trickling down the pane
Down the pane down the pane
The rain is trickling down the pane
Oh will it never stop.

When the children are able to perform the song fairly confidently and accurately, ask them to make downward movements with their hands on the words 'down the pane'. Each time the movement starts slightly lower than the previous one. Point out to them that these sections of the melody involve downward movement from one note to the next one below it in pitch. Therefore the melody, in these sections, is said to be 'moving downward by step'.

Draw the children's attention to the fact that, like the 'Celtic Lament' which they encountered earlier, this tune is again sung smoothly, i.e. legato.

Arrange the piano chart over the notes, so that Middle C corresponds to the note C nearest the centre of the piano. Draw the children's attention to the fact that, on the copymaster, there are four types of D:

D = the note immediately to the right of Middle C
D' = the next D above it.
D'' = the next one up again.
D, = the first D to the left of Middle C

You will find the notes indicated in this way on the piano chart.

Now ask four children to position themselves so that one child is opposite each of the Ds. Then, as the song is sung, each one plays his or her note on the appropriate beat. Another possibility is to ask two children to play – the first to play the top two Ds and the second to play the bottom two Ds. Alternatively you could arrange for one child to play all the Ds. Precisely which approach you adopt will depend on the abilities and experiences of the particular children with whom you are working.

Purpose
To help the children identify movement downward by step within a melody; to give them the opportunity to apply the knowledge of note positions on the piano, acquired in **Activity 35**.

Resources
Space for movement
Cassette: side 2, activity 36
Copymaster 41
Piano
Note position chart created from Copymasters 37 and 38 (see Activity 35).

Presentation
Start by teaching the children the words and tune of the following song.

Starting note: A
Count in: 1 2 3 4 1 2 3

37. RAIN COMPOSITION

Purpose
To give the children further experience of creating, notating and making audio-recordings of their own compositions; to give them the opportunity to perform each others' compositions; through performance and listening, to enable them to appreciate how a musical score can be interpreted in a variety of ways.

Resources
Copymaster 42. Make several copies of this, mount them onto card and cut them up so that each group has several copies of each symbol.
Range of pitched and unpitched instruments
Large sheets of paper and colouring pencils
Tape recorder

Presentation
Divide the children into groups. Give each group a mixture of pitched and unpitched percussion instruments. Discuss with them what happens when a storm builds up. It often starts with large, single drops of rain falling at fairly wide intervals. The speed and number then begin to increase, as does the sound. This might develop into a heavy downpour where the separate drops join together and you see a 'sheet' of water. There might be thunder and lightning at various times. The sound of the thunder and the amount of lightning will vary with each appearance. Then gradually, the rain subsides. The sound gets softer. The sheet of rain is replaced by separate drops. There might be short intervals when the drops stop altogether. Then the rain might seem to be starting again before further silences occur, single drops fall and finally the rainstorm disappears.

When they have discussed the possibilities, ask each group to decide on a particular sequence of events for its rain storm. Ask the children to work on various sounds to represent the various stages. As indicated in the introduction to this book, give them the opportunity to experiment with various possibilities, to play these to each other, to discuss and evaluate them and then to revise the ideas and combinations of ideas until a final version is reached.

When they reach this final stage, ask the children to use the pictures from the copymaster to represent the sounds which they have produced. This will involve both individual symbols and combinations of symbols. The larger pictures could represent louder sounds and the smaller pictures the softer sounds. They might wish to use colours to represent the instruments playing a particular symbol or combination of symbols. In some instances, more than one instrument might be playing the same idea.

When they have discussed these points and chosen their symbols, ask each group to perform to the rest of the class. At this point, they might wish to make tape recordings of the performances and draw final scores of the music. The advantage of the cards during the composition process is that they can be easily rearranged and this allows for redrafting. The final score, however, can be drawn on one large sheet.

Extension
As an extension to this work, the groups could swap scores and perform each other's work. This will enable them to appreciate the importance of producing clear scores for others to read. It will also show how even the most accurately written scores can allow for a wide range of interpretations of a composition. Discuss what differences you notice in terms of the speed, volume or mood of the successive performances.

38. OLD MOLLY HARE

Purpose
To teach the children a new song to which they can add an instrumental accompaniment; to give them further experience of performing and identifying one-beat and half-beat patterns; to introduce them to the use of the one beat rest and to enable them to convert sounds into signs and signs into sounds, using these symbols.

Resources
Cassette: side 2, activity 38
Copymaster 43
Chime bars D E F# G A

Presentation
Teach the children the following song, using the cassette, **Copymaster 43** and the suggestions included in the introduction to the book.

Starting note: A
Count in: 1 2 1 2

Old Molly Hare

1. Old Molly Hare (Sh!) What you doing
   there? (Sh!)
   Running through the cabbage patch as
   fast as I can tear (Sh!)

2. Old Molly Hare, what you doing there?
   Chewing chewing gum and making
   bubbles in the air.

3. Old Molly Hare, what you doing there?
   Sitting on a big broom stick and flying
   through the air.

As the children sing this song, make sure that, after the words 'Hare', 'there' and 'tear', they make a pointing movement and that there is a clear silence as they do so. To ensure that this silence is one beat in length, ask them to march on the spot as they sing and to take care that they do not let the previous sound spread into the silence.

When they are able to do this fairly confidently, add the chime bar accompaniment. As before, you could start by adding this yourself and then inviting the children to take turns in playing it.

You should also ask the singers to march on the spot as they perform, so that the beat is clear. This is particularly important for each silence (rest). An arm gesture in time with the beat of the foot will help ensure that each one is of the right length. As with earlier activities of this type, you will be far more confident in presenting it if you have worked out the patterns very carefully and thoroughly beforehand. Listening to the cassette frequently will help you with this.

Extension

Make several copies of the rest sign in the bottom right hand corner of **Copymaster 43**. Cut these out and mount on card. Together with the cards already created from **Copymaster 36**, the children should now be able to play games where they give each other various combinations of one-beat and half-beat sounds and one-beat rests to perform.

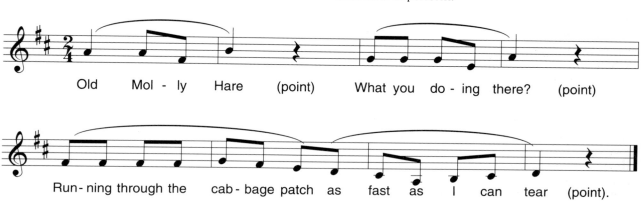

Old   Mol - ly   Hare   (point)   What you   do - ing   there?   (point)

Run - ning through the   cab - bage patch   as   fast   as   I   can   tear   (point).

39. DON'T STEP ON MY MUSICAL TOES

Purpose

To give the children further experience of improvising a percussion piece and of developing greater control in performance; to give them further experience of applying concepts of tempo and dynamics in performance.

Resources

A percussion instrument for every child in the group.
Copymasters 44 and 45

Presentation

Arrange the children in a circle on chairs. Under each child's chair put an instrument. Try to make the instruments as varied as possible and make sure that the instruments under adjacent chairs are as different from each other as possible. At a sign from you, ask the children to pick up the instruments and hold them very still. Starting with the child opposite you, and going round clockwise, ask each member of the circle to play one sound on her/his instrument.

When they have done this, ask them whether they actually produced one sound or more than one sound. The likelihood is that several children will have produced more than one sound, either because they had not concentrated on this part of the instruction or because they found it very difficult to produce only one sound on specific instruments such as bells or maracas.

Starting at a different point in the circle and possibly going in a different direction, repeat the activity, this time asking the children to be very careful to produce only one sound, or in the case of maracas, for example, as few sounds as possible.

You will probably find that, this second time round, the children will concentrate far more and the sounds will begin to take on more 'shape'. When they have mastered this, invite individual members of the class to act as the starters and to choose in which way the sound should travel.

Now tell the children that you are going to play the game again. This time, however, they must listen very carefully to the previous performer's sound and not come in until the very last vibration has died away. In other words they must not step on that person's musical toes! As soon as that person's sound has died they must come in with their sounds. This demands very careful listening and a quick response once they have established that the sound has gone entirely.

This time, you should find even greater levels of concentration developing in the pupils.

Extension 1
Play the above game again. This time, however, if a child's sound was originally loud, it should be made soft and vice versa. Again make sure that no one plays until the previous sound has died away completely.

Extension 2
Here the children should be asked to consider whether the original sound was long or short. If it was long, it should now be made short and vice versa.

Extension 3
The next step involves combining concepts. Thus a sound which was originally loud and long should now become soft and short. A sound which was originally short and loud should now be played long and softly, etc. Involve the children in discussing the type of sounds they produced and in finding the opposites each time.

Extension 4
For this activity, make copies of the volume and speed wheels on **Copymasters 44** and **45**. Mount them on cards, cut them out and then push a cocktail stick through the middle of each so that the wheel spins. The side on which it comes to rest will give a speed or volume indication. Start by giving all the children in the group a volume wheel. Ask them all to spin their wheels. Then, as the sound moves round the circle, they should play as loudly or as softly as indicated on their personal volume wheels. You could then do the same with the speed wheel before finally combining both.

You will find that the children will enjoy coming back to these activities again and again. They offer a wide range of possibilities which can be extended further by altering the number of times that the sound goes round the circle, the direction in which it travels, the number of children involved and the types and juxtaposition of instruments used. You could also extend the activity by arranging for more than one circle to perform at a time.

Whatever permutation you use, remember to ask the children to listen extremely carefully to the effect that they are producing. Give them the opportunity to discuss, criticise and refine their work and to make recordings of their pieces for further examination and development.

40. LEAP DOWN, JUMP DOWN

Purpose
To help the children perform and identify movement downward by leap within a melody; to enable them to add an instrumental melodic and chordal accompaniment to a sung melody.

Resources
Space for movement
Cassette: side 2, activity 40
Two sets of chime bars arranged:
    Set 1: D F# A D'
    Set 2: C# E G B
Copymaster 46

Presentation
Teach the children the words and music of the following song.

Starting note: D
Count in: 1 2 1 2

Leap Down, Jump Down

Leap down, jump down, land upon your toes.
Fall down, tumble down, land upon your nose.
Fly down, dive down, forget about your woes.
Now after all this leaping round go home and have a doze.

When the children can perform it fairly accurately and confidently, ask them to spread around the room and find a space where they will not bump into anybody else. Now ask them to experiment with various movements going from high to low. Encourage them to aim for as much variety as possible. Let them demonstrate their ideas to each other. Then give them the opportunity to perform the movements as they sing with the cassette.

When they have done this, discuss with them how the song gives the impression of leaping and jumping downwards. (It does this because of the large number of instances where the pitch of the melody moves downwards by leap from one note to another.)

You could refine the performance further by asking the children to sing more slowly at the end. Remind them, at this point, of the earlier work done on RALLENTANDO (Activities 27 and 39).

Extension

Now practise the accompaniment using **Copymaster 46**. For this, you will need two children, one on each of the sets of chime bars set out on the copymaster. As the first and third lines are sung, the first child should play the chime bars in time with the music, one on each beat in turn from right to left. On the second line, the second child should do the same with his/her chime bars. Then, on the final word, the first child should play the lower of the two notes in his/her set to provide a final chord. Do not be surprised if the children find this accompaniment too difficult at first. The song can be sung without it. Alternatively, you might decide to return to the song at a later point during the key stage and add the accompaniment to it then.

You could ask the children to make up further verses to the song, using their own words to emphasise the way that the tune progresses through downward melodic leaps.

41. SPRING SONG

Set 1: GBD
Set 2: D F# A
Set 3: D E F# G
Copymaster 47

Purpose

To teach the children a new song; to enable them to add a simple chordal and melodic accompaniment to the song; to give them further experience of performing and identifying rhythmic patterns involving two beat notes; and to help them identify the ABA pattern on which the form of the song is based.

Resources

Cassette: side 2, activity 41
Chime bars arranged into 3 sets:

Presentation

Using the tape, the copymasters and the suggested approaches in the introduction, teach the children the following song. In singing it, aim to give the song a light, bright feeling to reflect happiness at the arrival of spring. Encourage the children to sing confidently but not too loudly.

Starting note: D
Count in: 1 2 3 4 1 2 3 (NB The song starts on the last beat of the bar)

Spring Song

The winter snows are over Now welcome back the
  sun
The fields are clothed in clover Oh see the new
  lambs run.
The birds in every bower Are singing merrily
The buds give back their blessing To every branch
  and tree

When they can perform the words and the melody with a fair degree of confidence, draw the children's attention to the rhythm of the melody. This involves two-beat notes. Listen to the explanation of this on the cassette. By marching on the spot and clapping, help them to identify that the rhythmic pattern is as follows:

Line 1	da	da	da	da	da	da-	a	da	da	da	da	da	da	da-	a-	a	da
	4	1	2	3	4	1	2	3	4	1	2	3	4	1	2	3	4
Line 2		da	da	da	da	da-	a	da	da	da	da	da	da	da-	a-	a	di-di
		1	2	3	4	1	2	3	4	1	2	3	4	1	2	3	4
Line 3		da	da	da	di-di	da-	a	da	da	da	da	da	di-di	da-	a-	a	da
		1	2	3	4	1	2	3	4	1	2	3	4	1	2	3	4
Line 4		da	da	da	da	da-	a	da	da	da	da	da	da	da-	a-	a	
		1	2	3	4	1	2	3	4	1	2	3	4	1	2	3	

From here, you can move to helping them add the accompaniment. For this, you will need four children: two for each set of chime bars. In each case, one child in the pair should play the bottom note (G or D), while the other plays the top two notes (B and D or F# and A). As in earlier activities, make sure that the accompanists sing the song with the rest of the performers so that there is proper synchronisation.

When the tune and the chords are being played accurately, draw the children's attention to the pattern that underlies this song. Lines 1, 2 and 4 are the same as each other in terms of melody, rhythm and chords. The third line, however, is different; here the melody, rhythm and accompaniment are different from the rest of the song.

If we wanted to draw a diagram of the pattern of the song, it could look like this:

$$\Delta \quad \Delta \quad O \quad \Delta$$

Another way of describing patterns in music is to use letters. In this case we could say that the tune has a pattern of:

A A B A

Line 1 = A
Line 2 = A (because it is the same as the previous one)
Line 3 = B (because it is different)
Line 4 = A again (because the idea heard in line 1 comes back once more)

Explain to the children that the term which musicians give to patterns in music is FORM.

Extension
Explain that it is possible to have lots of different patterns in music and that as they learn new songs they will come across new patterns. They could also make up an improvisation with different forms.

The win - ter snows are o - ver Now wel - come back the sun. The

fields are clothed in clo - ver Oh see the new lambs run. The ___

birds in ev - ery ___ bow - er are sing - ing me - rri - ly. The

buds give back their ble - ssing to eve - ry branch and tree.

42. LISTENING TO FORMS IN MUSIC

Purpose
To extend the children's understanding of form in music and to give them practice in identifying different types of form.

Resources
Cassette: side 2, activity 42
Copymaster 48

Presentation
Ask the children to listen very carefully to the tunes and the descriptions of them given on the cassette. Play each one several times if necessary.

When they have had sufficient time to listen to the taped explanations, ask them to listen to the next track on the tape, to identify the pattern of each of the tunes played and then to circle their answers on the copymaster. The correct answers are shown on the following page:

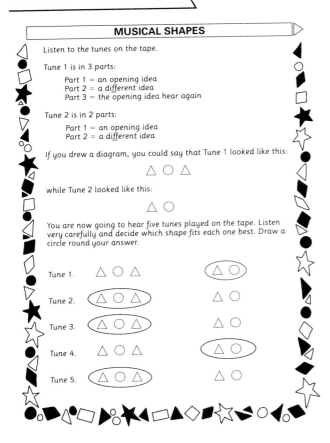

MUSICAL SHAPES

Listen to the tunes on the tape.

Tune 1 is in 3 parts:

    Part 1 = an opening idea
    Part 2 = a different idea
    Part 3 = the opening idea hear again

Tune 2 is in 2 parts:

    Part 1 = an opening idea
    Part 2 = a different idea

If you drew a diagram, you could say that Tune 1 looked like this:

△ ○ △

while Tune 2 looked like this:

△ ○

You are now going to hear five tunes played on the tape. Listen very carefully and decide which shape fits each one best. Draw a circle round your answer.

Tune 1.   △ ○ △   (△ ○)

Tune 2.   (△ ○ △)   △ ○

Tune 3.   (△ ○ △)   △ ○

Tune 4.   △ ○ △   (△ ○)

Tune 5.   (△ ○ △)   △ ○

43. IMPROVISING SHAPES

Purpose

To reinforce the children's understanding of the nature of form in music and to give them further experience of applying this understanding to improvisation activities.

Resources

Copymaster 49
Range of instruments

Presentation

Ask the children to think up a musical idea. When they have worked on this along the lines suggested in the section on Composition (p. 13), they can perform it. This becomes shape 1 on the Copymaster.

Now ask them to think of a contrasting idea. It could be different in terms of the instruments used, its melody or its volume. When the children have experimented with this idea and refined it, help them to add it to the first idea to create shapes 2 and 3.

Extension

From here the children can progress to devising more complex patterns, based on the collection of shapes at the foot of **Copymaster 49**.

44. THE TRUMPET IS SOUNDING

Purpose

To teach the children to sing a simple song which can be performed as a canon in three parts; to enable them to add simple chordal accompaniments to the song; to draw their attention to the use of leaps and stepwise movement in the melody; and to enable them to listen for balance of volume as they perform within groups and as a whole ensemble.

Resources

Cassette: side 2, activity 44
Copymasters 50 and 51
Two sets of chime bars:

58

Set 1: E F# A
Set 2: C# D
Arrange these as indicated on Copymaster 51.

Presentation

Teach the children the following song, making sure that they do not rush the quicker notes, particularly in the last two lines:

Starting note: A
Count in: 1 2 3 1 2

The Trumpet is Sounding

The trumpet is sounding,
Its echo rebounding
*
To greet the dawning
And break of the day
To greet the dawning
And break of the day.

When the children have performed it a few times and can sing it fairly confidently, draw their attention to the way that the melody is constructed. In lines 1 to 4, the melody moves mainly by leaps from one note to another. In lines 5 and 6, however, it moves mainly by steps. To reinforce this ask the children, when they are singing, to make hand movements which show the jerky, jumping movements in the first four lines and the smoother movements in the last two lines.

The next stage is to add the accompaniment. Ask all the instrumentalists to clap out the following rhythmic pattern, based on one- and two-beat note patterns:

2	1	2	1	2	1	2	1
da-a	da	da-a	da	da-a	da	da-a	da

Arrange the two sets of chime bars as indicated on **Copymaster 50**.

Group 1   Group 2   Group 2   Group 1

Practise the patterns with the players, making sure that they play on the appropriate beat. As before, remember that this will best be done by asking the performers to sing as they play.

Extension

From here you can progress to teaching the children to sing the song as a canon. Divide your class firstly into two groups. The first group should start to sing. Then the second group should enter as the first group sings the note marked with an asterisk. Remember to encourage the children to listen not only to themselves or to their own group but also to the singing of the second group. This will help make the performance a musical one and prevent its becoming a shouting match.

When this has been mastered, add the chordal accompaniment already learnt. To allow for the fact that there is a second group of singers, it will be necessary to play the pattern at the bottom of **Copymaster 50**.

an extra time. You could also play this pattern at the very beginning as an introduction before the first group of singers enters.

Next add a third group of singers and ask them to enter when the first group has reached the point marked † on the diagram. To produce a satisfactory performance, start with the same introduction as before. Then ask the instrumentalists to keep playing until the last voice has finished and then to round off with one more playing of the pattern on the copymaster.

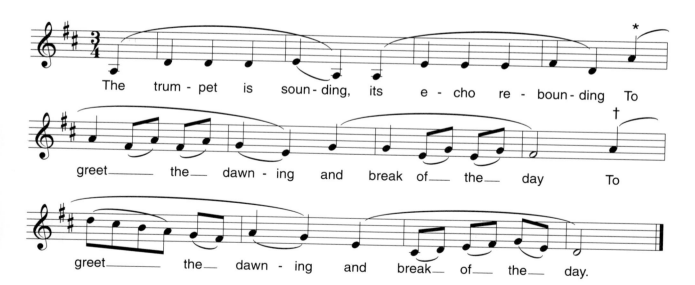

45. JOHN PEEL

Purpose

To give the children further experience of singing a song based on a verse and chorus pattern; to introduce them to the significance of the pause sign in music; to give them further experience of applying the indication 'rallentando' and to introduce them to the meaning of 'a tempo'; to enable them to add a simple accompaniment to the song learnt; and to give them further experience of listening to the sound of brass instruments.

Resources

Cassette: side 3, activity 45
Copymasters 52 and 53
Chime bars: E♭, A♭ and B♭
Space for movement

Presentation

Start by teaching the children the following song:

Starting note: G
Count in: 1 2 3 4 1 2 3 (NB The first word is sung on the 4th beat of the bar.)

John Peel

1. D'ye ken John Peel with his coat so gay?
   D'ye ken John Peel at the break of the day?
   D'ye ken John Peel when he's far far away
   With his hounds and his horn in the morning?

Chorus

   For the sound of his horn brought me from my bed
   And the cry of his hounds which he oft-times led,
   Peel's 'Haloo' would awaken the dead,
   Or the fox from his lair in the morning

2. Then here's to John Peel, from my heart and soul,
   Let's drink to his health, let's finish the bowl;
   We'll follow John Peel through fair and through foul,
   If we want a good hunt in the morning.

Chorus

   For the sound of his horn etc.

3. D'ye ken John Peel with his coat so gay?
   He lived at Troutbeck once on a day;
   Now he has gone far, far away,
   We shall never hear his voice in the morning.

Chorus

   For the sound of his horn etc.

When the children can sing the first verse fairly fluently, draw their attention to the **rallentando** sign over the words 'ken John Peel when he's far far away'. Remind them of its meaning from an earlier activity (rallentando = getting gradually slower). Practice the music as far as the end of that line. Then explain to the children that when you wish to return to the original speed, you use the term **'a tempo'**. Also draw their attention to the sign over the syllable 'loo'. Explain to them that this sign is used in music to show when the note should be held for longer than normal. The term used to describe it is a **pause**.

Perform the whole of the verse, applying these terms and producing changes of speed accordingly. When this has been mastered, divide the class into two groups, one of which should be larger than the other. Now ask the smaller of the two groups to sing the verse and the larger group to sing the chorus. Alternatively, you could invite an individual child to sing the verse as a solo while the rest of the class sings the chorus. Remind the children of other songs encountered in this book which are based on a verse–chorus pattern (e.g. Blow the Man Down).

Play the music through on the tape again and this time draw the children's attention to the sound of the horn. Explain to them that hunters use horns to indicate to the rest of the group where the fox is so that everyone can travel in the right direction.

Extension

From here you can progress to adding the chime bar accompaniment to the syllables indicated on **Copymaster 53**. As in other activities of this type, remind the instrumental performers to sing along with the rest so that their accompaniment is correctly synchronised with the vocal line. You could start by adding the accompaniment yourself and then teaching individual children to play it. The next stage is to ask the children to try the listening puzzle on Copymaster 53. The answers are given on the cassette.

As you can see this activity includes several learning points. Do not try to present them all in one go. Instead, return to this activity several times to consolidate one point and then to introduce another. Do not expect every child to be able to perform all the activities. Several have been included to ensure that there is an appropriate challenge for children of varying abilities in your class.

Verse
D' ye ken John Peel with his coat so gay? D' ye ken John Peel at the

rallentando   *a tempo*
break of the day? D' ye ken John Peel when he's far far a-way With his

Chorus
hounds and his horn in the morn - ing? For the sound of his horn brought

me from my bed And the cry of his hounds which he oft-times led,

Peel's 'Ha-loo!' would a-wa-ken the dead, Or the fox from his lair in the morn-ing.

46. THE BRITISH GRENADIERS

Purpose
To give the children further practice in moving in time to the underlying beat of a song; to enable them to identify the way that the beats in this song are arranged into groups of two; to enable them to add a simple unpitched and pitched instrumental accompaniment to the song; to enable them to apply their developing understanding of notation to the performance of these accompaniments; to give them further practice in recording, listening to and criticising their own performances; to make the children aware of the features in a performance which give a piece a particular character or mood.

Resources
Cassette: side 3, activity 46
Tambour, drum, claves
Piano chart (Copymasters 37 and 38) arranged as indicated in Activity 35

Two sets of chime bars:
    Set 1: C F
    Set 2: F, F
(Arrange these as indicated in Copymaster 54)
Space for movement
Copymasters 54–56

Presentation
Start by teaching the children the following song, using
the cassette, **Copymasters 55** and **56** and the suggestions
contained in the introduction to help you:

Starting note: C
Count in: 1 2 1 (NB The first note starts on the second
beat of the bar.)

The British Grenadiers

Some talk of Alexander
And some of Hercules
Of Hector and Lysander
And such great names as these
But of all the world's great heroes
There's none that can compare
With a tow row row row row row row
To the British Grenadier.

When the children can perform the melody and words
fairly accurately, ask them to march in time to the
music. They could either do this on the spot or by
moving around the room. Next, ask them to clap on the
beat marked | each time. Some of the children could
then be given claves to play on this first beat each time.

The next stage is to invite one of the children to add
the lower accompaniment line, i.e. the one involving
the regular pattern:

F, F

From here, you can progress to asking the children to
read and clap the rhythmic pattern written below the
beat numbers:

| ⊓ | |
da di-di da   da

When the rhythm is being clapped accurately, transfer
the pattern to the two chime bars C & F to produce the
following:

| ⊓ | |
da di-di da   da
F   F F   C   C

Now perform the song again, with the whole of the
pitched and unpitched percussion added.

Listen to the performance on the tape and discuss with the children what makes this sound like military music. Draw their attention to such features as the use of the drums and the trumpets and the very confident way in which the song is performed.

At various points in the activity, or at the end, record the children's performance. Then play it back to them and discuss the effect. Use the questions on **Copymaster 56** to prompt you in this and to help the children themselves to complete the sheet. You could ask them to comment on successive performances of the music as it is built up to see if the comments change over time. You could then use the sheets as a basis for a display with a title such as 'How Our Performance Improved.'

47. IMPROVISATION BASED ON THE SIGNS RALLEN-TANDO, ACCELERANDO, A TEMPO AND PAUSE

Purpose
To give the children the opportunity to select and respond to varying speed indications during improvisations.

Resources
An instrument for each child in the class
Copymaster 57

Presentation
Make copies of **Copymaster 57**, mount it onto card, then cut it into four signs. Attach a handle of tough cardboard or plywood to the back of each sign.

The children take an instrument each and sit in a circle. One child takes the role of the conductor. He or she has the tempo signs and holds these up at various times. The performers then have to react accordingly. The conductor should try various combinations and the children should discuss which ones are most effective. They should then reproduce, practise and refine the effects. Gradually a composition can be built up in this way.

You could progress to asking two conductors to direct two groups as they perform. The children should then also think in terms of varying the volumes, possibly using the indicators from earlier activities, e.g. **Copymaster 14**.

Extension
They could further extend the work to include a consideration of varying musical shapes, using **Copymaster 49**.

48. PLAYING THE BLACK KEYS ON THE PIANO

Resources
Copymasters 58, 59, 37 and 38
Piano

Presentation
Revise Activity 35 so that the children are fully acquainted with the positioning of the white notes on the piano. Then explain that, now that they have learnt the names of the white notes, they are going to be taught the names of the black notes.

Ask them to show you Middle C. The black note immediately to the right of that C is called C sharp (written C#). In the same way, the black note immediately to the right of D is called D sharp (D#) and the ones immediately to the right of F G and A are called F sharp (F#), G sharp (G#) and A sharp (A#) respectively.

Now ask them to find the notes on **Copymaster 58**. When they have mastered this, tell them that each black note also has another name. To explain this, ask them to look at the note D. There is a black note immediately to the left of this. This note, they already know as C sharp. But it can also be called D flat (written D♭). In the same way, the note immediately to the left of E is known as

Purpose
To enable the children to apply the piano chart to the identification of sharp and flat notes on the keyboard and to apply this knowledge to the playing of a simple tune involving the black keys.

63

E♭ and the ones to the left of G, A and B are known as G♭, A♭ and B♭ respectively.

Check the positions of these on the piano.

Now ask the children to find the notes indicated on **Copymaster 59**. When they can do so, ask them to give you an alternative name for each of the following:

F# =	C# =
E♭ =	A# =
G♭ =	B♭ =

etc.

It is because these black notes have two names that sometimes chime bars have two indications stamped on them.

As with several other activities in this book, do not expect to be able to cover all this information in one go. Give the children time to develop their understanding and to practise their skills of note identification. Do not feel that the children have got to master this information before they progress to the next activities but it will help to develop the children's knowledge further and this type of activity can be used to challenge those who are progressing at a faster rate than others.

Remember that the knowledge presented here is a means to an end and should be developed through application to the practical activities in the book and should not be viewed as an end in itself with no attempt to apply it to performance.

49. COME PACK YOUR CARES AWAY!

Purpose

To give the children further experience of moving in time to the underlying beat of a song, of marking the accented beats and of adding a pitched percussion accompaniment to it; to enable them to identify how the beats in the song are arranged into patterns of three (a metre of three); to give them the opportunity to listen to similar metrical arrangements in other pieces of music; to give them experience of identifying an AABA pattern in a melody.

Resources

Cassette: side 3, activity 49
Copymasters 60 and 61
Two sets of chimebars
    Set 1: F G
    Set 2: A, E
Bass xylophone notes C, & F, (if you do not have this instrument available, use a third set of chime bars). Arrange the above as indicated in Copymaster 60.

Presentation

Start by teaching the children the words and tune to the following song:

Starting note: C
Count in: 1 2 3 1 2 3

Come, Pack Your Cares Away!

Come pack your cares away
Come let us dance and play

This is a special holiday
Come pack your cares away
Come let us dance and play
This is a special holiday
Come listen to the band
Come hold your partner's hand
Slap and clap the length of the day
Come pack your cares away
Come let us dance and play
This is a special holiday

In teaching this song, pay particular attention to making sure that the children do not rush the move from the second to the third notes in each bar.

When they can sing the song fairly confidently and accurately, ask the children to tap out the beat gently and regularly on their laps. From here, you can progress to accenting the first beat of each bar by stamping on the floor as well as tapping the beat. Alternatively, mark each beat with a different gesture, e.g.:

Beat	1	2	3
Gesture	Knee Slap	Clap	Clap

or

Beat	1	2	3
Gesture	Knee Slap	Clap	Snap

Draw the children's attention to the fact that the beats in this song are arranged into groups of three or, to give it its technical term, into a **metre** of three. In such cases, the first beat is the loudest, the second is less loud and

64

the third beat is the softest. The types of movement used, particularly in the last arrangement of gestures, reflects this.

Ask the children to listen to the tunes on the cassette. In some of these, the beats are arranged into a metre of three and in others into a metre of two. Ask the children to make appropriate movements in time to the beat of the music, as indicated by the presenter on the tape.

Now draw the children's attention to the way that this tune is constructed. It has a pattern of:

A = From line 1 to line 3 of the words

A = line 4 to line 6

B = line 7 to line 9

A = line 10 to line 12

Extension

The next stage is to enable the children to add a pitched accompaniment to the song, using copymasters 60 and 61. Start this by asking the bass xylophone player to perform the bottom line in the accompaniment.

Practise the top line of the accompaniment with the first chime bar player. Then ask that player to join with the bass xylophone player to play the accompaniment as the others sing. Do this slowly at first and make sure that the two performers are counting '1 2 3' regularly so that their notes coincide with the appropriate beat. They

could start by saying the beats. Then, as they practise, they could whisper the beats and then finally think them. But they must not forget to think them otherwise their hands will dictate the speed and the whole performance will become very ragged. When the bass xylophone player and first chime bar player have gained some confidence, add the second chime bar part, applying the same principles as those already outlined.

Do not expect this activity to be easy. It will take time, effort and practise for the accompanists to perform together accurately. Give them the opportunity to learn their parts individually. Then let them perform together very slowly as you tap out the beat and they say, whisper and think it. Let them practise in various combinations:

> xylophone and chime bar 1
> xylophone and chime bar 2
> chime bars 1 and 2
> xylophone, chime bars 1 and 2
> each of the above combinations with and without the vocal part.

Start slowly and gradually build up speed.

Remember that, as with the other sections of this book, all the activities cannot be pursued in one go. You will need to take time over them and return to them to consolidate the activities. In some instances, you might feel that you will need to build up your own musical confidence before embarking on the activity. But

Come pack your cares a-way, Come let us dance and play, This is a spe-cial ho-li-day. ho-li-day. Come lis-ten to the band, Come hold your part-ner's hand, Slap___ and clap___ the length of the day. Come pack your cares a-way. Come let us dance and play. This is a spe-cial ho-li-day.

remember the best way of building confidence is to do it gradually and not expect it all to be perfect immediately.

You are now in a position to bring all these elements together into a performance involving the children singing and marking the beats with knee slaps, claps and finger snaps, and with the addition of the two types of pitched instrumental accompaniment.

50. PLAINCHANT

Purpose

To teach the children to sing a short plainchant melody from the medieval period; to enable them to listen to plainchant music (which does not make use of a regular beat); to enable them to identify the difference between music which makes use of a regular beat and that which does not; to give them further experience of using movements to indicate the rise and fall of a melody and to identify mainly step-wise melodic movement; to introduce them to medieval church music and to the music of Hildegard of Bingen.

Resources

Cassette: side 3, activity 50
Copymaster 62

Presentation

Play the plainchant on the cassette several times and ask the children to listen carefully to it. Ask them to listen to it again and, this time, to draw the shape of the music in the air by raising and lowering their arms very smoothly as the pitch of the music goes up and down. When they have done this a few times, ask them whether the music moves smoothly or whether it has lots of notes which jump around. (The melody is very smooth and makes little use of leaps.)

Now teach them to sing the plainchant. Focus particularly on making sure that the melody is sung very smoothly and that the children breathe at the ends of phrases, as indicated on page 5, and not half-way through a phrase. (NB Although the melody does not have a regular underlying beat, the count of 1-2-3-4 has been included on the cassette to ensure that the pupils start together when they sing. You can use this for the same reason but make sure that you do not keep to a rigid beat during the performance, otherwise the effect of this type of music will be lost.)

Start by singing the whole melody to 'la' or 'coo'. When the children have gained confidence in doing this, teach them the words. Explain to them that the words which they are singing are in an ancient language called Latin. Draw their attention to the meaning of the words on the copymaster by means of the translation:

O ignis spiritus paracliti,
vita vite omnis creature,
sanctus es vivificando formas.

Sanctus es ungendo
periculose fractos;
sanctus es tergendo
fetida vulnera

O fire of the benevolent Spirit,
the living life of all Creation,
you are holy in giving life to all.

You are holy in caring
for all who are sick;
you are holy in tending
their painful wounds.

When they are able to sing the plainsong fairly confidently, ask them to listen to the tape again, paying particular attention to the way that the words are pronounced and where the singers breathe. Then ask them to sing along with the voices on the tape. Emphasise the importance of performing this music in a very relaxed way.

Draw the children's attention to the fact that most of the music to which they have listened up until now has had a clear underlying beat. How have they known this? (Because, as they have sung the songs, they have been able to make regular movements in time to it such as marching, walking, pulling etc.) Could they make similar regular movements to the music which they have just heard? (No. If they are in doubt about this, play the music again and let them try to produce regular movements in time to it. The movements which they produced when drawing the shape of the tune earlier were not regular.) Let the children attempt the Listenzing Puzzle at the bottom of copymaster 62.

Who do they think is performing the music which they have heard? (A group of female singers.) Where do they think it is being performed? (In a church.) The pupils might not all have the experience to be able to give these answers. In that case, you will need to point out to them that this music is sung in a church by a group of nuns. Explain how nuns are groups of women who live together in one building called a convent or a nunnery and devote themselves to worshipping God through prayer and music, and sometimes also through teaching, running hospitals, doing social work, etc.

Background information

The plainsong on the cassette was written by a composer called Hildegard of Bingen, who was born in Germany in 1098. She was educated in a convent school, where she excelled in science, history, literature and music. She became a nun and then an abbess, and soon began to write books, plays and music of her own. She also received visions where, she said, God spoke directly to her and helped her in her work. Her many talents made her so famous that some of the most important kings, emperors and leaders of the church in Europe at the time came to Hildegard for advice.

In 1147, she and the other nuns moved to another part of Germany, to a place called Bingen on the river Rhine. Because of this, Hildegard became known as Hildegard of Bingen.

At this point, explain to the children that they are going to hear a number of melodies being played on the cassette. They must listen very carefully and decide whether the tunes have got a regular beat or not. They should circle their answers on the copymaster each time. The answers are as follows: No. 1 = No beat, No. 2 = Beat, No. 3 = Beat, No. 4 = No beat.

51. BELLS AND CARILLONS

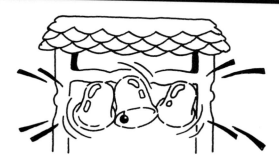

Purpose

To teach the children a short song which can be sung and played in canon; to enable them to add a chordal accompaniment to this and to apply their developing understanding of notation in performing the music.

Resources

Cassette: side 3, activity 51
Two sets of the following chime bars: D E F# G A D'
Metallophone: Remove all bars except the following: D F# A. (Alternatively, you could highlight those notes with removable stickers.)
Copymaster 63

Presentation

Start by teaching the children the words and tune of the following song:

Starting note: D
Count in: 1 2 1 2

Listen to the Carillon

Listen to the carillon*
Its merry bells resounding
Hear from every hill and vale
Its echoing sound rebounding

When the children can perform this fairly accurately, invite two of them to add the chord D F# A on the beats marked 1 each time on the copymaster. One child should play the D while the second child should play the other two notes. As before, make sure that the performers also sing the song, so that they synchronise their chord with the melody.

Now ask the class to march on the spot and to clap out the rhythm of the syllables as they sing. Remind them that one sound per beat = da and two sounds per beat = di-di. Then help them to apply this information to deciphering the rhythm of the song which is:

Lis- ten to the car-i- llon its me - rry bells re - soun-ding

di - di di-di di-di di - di di -di di -di da   da

Hear from ev-ery hill and vale its echo-ing sounds re-boun-ding

di - di   di -di di - di   di - di di - di di -   di da   da

Now ask some of the children to practise applying this rhythm to the performance of the melody on the chime bars. Start by asking them to practise alone, then let them play together (this will take time, so you will need to make allowances for it).

The children can now sing the song and play the melody, as well as the chords, on the chime bars.

Extension 1

When the children can perform the above effectively, try performing the music in canon. You could start by dividing the class into three groups: two groups of singers and one group playing the chords. Ask the chord players to play two chords at the beginning of the piece as an introduction and two chords after the last voice has finished in order to give it a sense of completion. This, of course, will be in addition to playing while the singers perform.

The first group of singers should start. Then, at the point where they are singing the syllable marked with an asterisk (*), the second group of singers should enter.

Extension 2

Ask the performers on the two sets of chime bars to play the melody together. Then practise performing it as a canon, with the second chime bar player starting at the point marked with an asterisk. This could be added to the chordal accompaniment to produce an instrumental version of the music.

Extension 3

When the children have mastered all the above, try putting the whole texture together so that you have two sets of singers in canon, two chime bar performers playing in canon and a chordal accompaniment supporting it all.

Obviously, there are many activities subsumed within this overall activity. Do not expect to be able to cover them all in one go. Return to the activity from time to time and develop it using the suggestions in the Extension section. The amount that you will be able to cover will vary according to the abilities and experiences of the children with whom you are working.

List - en to the ca - ri - llon, its me - rry bells re - sound - ing.

Hear from eve - ry hill and vale, its echo - ing sound re - bound - ing.

52. CHIME COMPOSITION ▶

Purpose

To give the children the opportunity to listen to clock chimes; to make up their own chimes; to notate them and perform those composed by fellow pupils.

Resources

Cassette: side 3, activity 52
Copymasters 64 and 65
Chime bars: D E F# G A B

Presentation

Play the children the recording of the Westminster Chimes on the cassette. Ask them whether they recognise it and where they have heard it before. Now teach them to play the tune, using **Copymaster 64**.

Next ask the children to take turns in making up their own chimes, using the chime bars provided. When they have tried it out several times, refined it and decided on a final version, ask them to write the letter names for the tune on **Copymaster 65**. They could then swap scores and play each other's tunes. By doing so, they will be putting their notation skills to practical use. Through careful listening, they will also be able to check on the accuracy of their own and others' performance and notational skills.

53. WOODWIND SOUNDS

Purpose
To help children understand the basis of sound production with woodwind instruments; to enable them to understand that the greater the length of a tube, the lower the sound it produces; to give them further experience of listening to woodwind instruments and to music from the medieval period.

Resources
Cassette: side 3, activity 53
Number of empty, narrow-necked bottles of different sizes
Copymaster 66

Presentation
Ask the children to blow across the top of the bottles to produce a sound. When they can do this, ask them to play a variety of bottles. What do they notice about the pitch of the sounds produced by the bottles? (The larger the bottle, the lower the pitch of the sound produced.)

Explain to them that it is the volume of air in the bottle that is important. The greater the volume of air, the lower the sound. To show this, take one of the bottles and blow across it and notice the pitch of the sound produced. Now pour a certain amount of water into the bottle and blow across it again. The pitch of the note produced should now be higher. The pouring of further amounts of water will raise the pitch even more.

Explain that on instruments like the flute, the sound is produced by blowing across a mouth piece in much

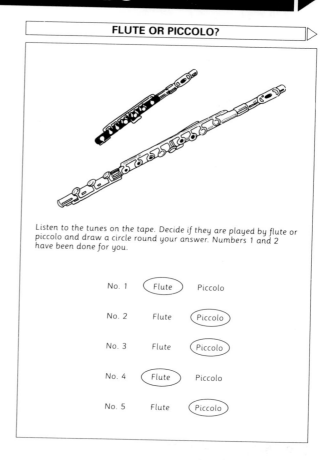

FLUTE OR PICCOLO?

Listen to the tunes on the tape. Decide if they are played by flute or piccolo and draw a circle round your answer. Numbers 1 and 2 have been done for you.

No. 1   (Flute)   Piccolo

No. 2   Flute   (Piccolo)

No. 3   Flute   (Piccolo)

No. 4   (Flute)   Piccolo

No. 5   Flute   (Piccolo)

the same way as one produces a sound with a bottle. The smaller the tube of the instrument, the higher the pitch of the sounds.

Now play them the examples of flute and piccolo tunes on the cassette. When they have listened, ask them which they think is the smaller instrument. Then tell them that the first sound was produced by a flute and the second by a piccolo.

Explain to them that they are now going to listen to a series of tunes, some played by the flute and some by the piccolo. They must decide which is which in each case and circle their answers on the copymaster.

Remind the children of the work already done on medieval church music (Activity 50). Explain to them that it was not only in church that music was performed at this time. It was also played to accompany dances. Play them the example on the cassette.

54. REED INSTRUMENTS

Purpose
To extend the children's understanding of how wood-wind instruments operate by introducing them to the notion of reed instruments; to enable them to identify, and differentiate between, tunes played on the clarinet, oboe and the bassoon.

Resources
Cassette: side 3, activity 54
Blades of grass

Copymaster 67

Presentation
Take the blade of grass as shown in the diagram. Make sure that it is very tight.

Now blow between the thumbs. This should produce a high squeeking sound. Let the children experiment with making their own sounds in this way.

Explain to the children that the sound which you hear is the result of the air rushing across the blade of grass and making it vibrate. The same principle is used in certain woodwind instruments. But there, instead of a blade of grass, a small piece of bamboo is used. This is attached to a mouthpiece. As the performer blows on it, the reed begins to vibrate and make a sound. This sound is then made louder (or amplified) by the fact that it is attached to a pipe which acts as an echo chamber. This is what happens in the case of the clarinet, for example.

From here you can go on to explain to the children that, in the case of some instruments, two reeds are used. These are tied together and, as the air goes over them, they vibrate against each other to produce a sound which is again made louder by the pipe which acts as an echo chamber. Two instruments which make use of double reeds of this type are the oboe and the bassoon, both of which are pictured on **Copymaster 67**. Ask the children to look at these pictures and tell you which one they think will play the lowest notes. (The lowest notes will be produced by the larger of the two instruments, i.e. the bassoon. Draw their attention to the fact that, because of its size, the section holding the reed has to be bent to enable the performer to put it into his or her mouth.)

Play them the examples of oboe and bassoon tunes on the cassette to help the children gain familiarity with the sounds.

To prevent confusion, you might find it better to introduce each of the instruments in this activity separately. Precisely how you time it will depend on the ability and experiences of the children with whom you are working.

55. GOLDEN SLUMBERS

Bass xylophone notes: C D G. If there is no bass xylophone available use a higher pitched xylophone. The wooden sound will give a more mellow sound than a metal instrument and will reflect the character and mood of the lullaby.
Tambour

Presentation
Start by teaching the words and tune of the following song to the class.

Starting note: D
Count in: 1 2 3 1 2 3

Golden Slumbers

Golden slumbers kiss your eyes
Smiles awake you when you rise
Sleep pretty maiden do not cry
And I will sing a lullaby.

When the children can sing it fairly confidently, ask them to sing the first line, while you clap the beat or tap it out on the tambour. On the basis of the rhythmic work already done, they should be able to work out that the first bar consists of one note which lasts for two beats and another which lasts for 1 beat (da-a da). This pattern is heard three times. On the word 'eyes', however, the note is sung for three beats: da-a-a.

Now help the children to identify where else there are notes which last for three beats. You will hear them on 'rise' and 'by'.

With the aid of the copymaster, show them that a three-beat note is represented by the following symbol:

Purpose
To give the children further experience of performing phrases smoothly, of producing an even, soft sound when singing and of performing music in which the beats are arranged in groups of three (triple metre); to enable them to read rhythmic patterns which involve the use of crotchets, minims and dotted minims; to enable them to differentiate between woodwind instruments on the basis of their sounds.

Resources
Cassette: side 3, activity 55
Copymasters 68 and 69

♩. . Draw their attention to the dot after the note which makes it 1 1/2 times as long as a note without the dot.

You can now concentrate further on the melody. The important point here is to ensure that the children sing each phrase smoothly in one breath. When they take breaths between phrases ask them to do so as quietly as possible, so that the effect is not spoilt by great gasps for air. Also encourage them to sing softly and evenly throughout the piece. But remember that, just because they are singing softly, their words should not become inaudible. Encourage them to pronounce their consonants clearly. Revise the activities described on pages 4 and 5 of the Introduction to help them with this. Also, encourage them to sing the whole song in a relaxed way, without rushing it. Remind them that this is a lullaby not a dance.

When the children have learnt to sing the song and can perform it fairly fluently, add the instrumental accompaniment indicated on **Copymaster 68**. Start by adding the accompaniment yourself and then invite some of the children to perform it.

Explain to the children that there are three versions of the song on the tape, in addition to the one involving the singers. One version is played by a bassoon, another by the clarinet and the third by the oboe. Ask the children to listen to them carefully and mark on **Copymaster 69** which instrument is playing each time. The answers are shown opposite:

LISTENING PUZZLE 6

You will hear the tune of 'Golden Slumbers' being played three times. Each time a different instrument will be playing it. Draw a circle round the name of the instrument which you think is playing. It will either be a clarinet, an oboe or a bassoon.

1. (clarinet)   oboe   bassoon

2. clarinet   (oboe)   bassoon

3. clarinet   oboe   (bassoon)

Gol - den slum - bers kiss your eyes. Smiles— a -

wake you when you rise. Sleep pre - tty mai - den

do— not cry— And I will sing a lul - la - by.

56. LONDON'S BURNING

Purpose

To give children further experience of performing in a mixed vocal and instrumental ensemble and of adding rhythmic ostinati on pitched and unpitched percussion instruments; to give them experience of preparing a performance and making decisions about how to organise and direct it; to enable them to explore the range of possibilities available in the preparation, presentation and recording of a performance; to develop their understanding of the concepts of accompaniment, texture, ostinato and balance.

Resources

Chime bars: D E G A B C' D'
Notes G and D on bass metallophone. (Alternatively, these notes could be played on two chime bars or on another xylophone or glockenspiel.)
Unpitched percussion instruments, e.g. drum or tambour
Copymaster 70
Cassette: side 3, activity 56

Presentation

Start by reminding the children of the rounds and canons which they have already sung. Tell them that they are now going to perform a very well known canon. Then teach the melody and words to the children.

Starting note = D
Count in: 1 2 3 1 2

London's Burning

London's burning, London's burning,
Fetch the engines, fetch the engines,
Fire! Fire! Fire! Fire!
Pour on water, pour on water.

When they have mastered this, ask one or two children to say the rhythm of the opening words 'London's burning' (di-di da da) over and over and then to clap the rhythm as they say it. This can then be transferred onto an unpitched instrument such as a drum or tambour and played as an accompaniment throughout the performance.

A further accompanimental idea can be produced by asking another small group to say and clap the rhythm of 'Fire! Fire!' (da da-a da da-a). This can again be transferred to an unpitched instrument and played with the other singers and performers.

These accompaniments could be played as the performers sing the round. Each new voice should enter when the previous one is singing the word marked with the asterisk.

Extension

The performance could be further extended in the following ways. When the children are able to sing the song with confidence, add the pitched instrumental accompaniment from **Copymaster 70**. You could start by adding the accompaniment yourself, then asking one of the class to take over this part.

You could also teach some of the children to play the tune as well as the accompaniment. Make sure that, as each accompanying part is added, you check the balance of the overall performance to ensure that the vocal part is not drowned out. Remember that an accompaniment should be a support and that each instrument might need to play more softly as each new part is added.

Discuss the effects with the pupils and decide how the final performance could be arranged. There are many possibilities available to you. The following is one:

Section 1: Pitched percussion accompaniment starts. After a few bars the voices enter and sing the melody through once.
Section 2: Pitched percussion continues. This time the unpitched percussion accompaniments are added to them and play for a few bars.
Section 3: The pitched and unpitched percussion from section 2 continue to play as the song is now sung in canon.
Section 4: As each voice finishes, the instruments get softer and softer. Alternatively, they could stop playing one by one until only one voice remains to be heard.

Remember that this is only a suggestion. Try out and discuss the effects of other possibilities with your pupils. Then, when you have decided on the most satisfactory version, practise it and present a performance of it to the rest of the class or to other classes in the school. You could also make a recording of the performance which might be 'broadcast' to the rest of the school as part of a school 'radio programme' or made available in the library for others to hear it.

73

57. FIRE COMPOSITION

misery and fear. Alternatively, they might refer to a building going up in flames and the panic and terror which this can arouse. There will no doubt be further ideas which you and the children can suggest.

Divide the pupils into groups. Each group will be asked to create the impression of the type of fire and associated feelings which they have chosen as a result of the preceding discussion. Make sure that not everyone has chosen the same type of fire. If you feel that there is a danger of this, then assign specific groups to particular tasks.

Start by giving each group time to experiment with the different types of sounds which can be produced by the paper. If the pupils are stuck for ideas, suggest the following:

- crumpling up the paper quickly;
- tearing the paper very slowly into strips (this can actually be done in such a way as to create a rhythmic pattern if you so wish);
- flapping the paper;

Of course, the sound effect produced even by one approach will vary considerably according to the texture of the paper being used.

When the pupils have experimented with the possible effects, invite each group to work on its composition, organising the activity along the lines suggested in the section on composition on pages 13–16.

Groups should work on their own compositions and listen to and comment on each other's emerging compositions. Then, when they have redrafted their creations and arrived at the point where they are happy with the effects they are trying to produce, let them perform their compositions to each other.

At this point, you could arrange for the results to be recorded and made into part of the class's folio of compositions which can be played to parents, other pupils and visitors to the school.

Purpose

To give the children the opportunity to create compositions based on the theme of fire; to extend their awareness of the way in which music can be given pattern and shape and to give them the opportunity to listen to and discuss the way that a composer can use instruments to convey the effects of fire; to encourage them to reflect on and modify their own compositions in the light of their listening experiences.

Resources

A wide range of different types of paper, e.g. sheets of newspaper, pages from glossy magazines, cellophane paper, grease-proof paper, foil etc.
Tape recorder

Presentation

You might wish to start this activity by presenting a performance of the round rehearsed in Activity 56 or you might want to go straight into the discussion. Talk with the children about what different forms of fire there might be and what types of reactions these stir up in people. They might mention a log fire in a house and the feeling of warmth and comfort which this can produce. They might mention a fire lit by people in distress who are trying to keep themselves alive and draw others' attention to their plight. Such a fire is likely to be associated with feelings of unhappiness,

Extension

You might find that, when the compositions have been completed, there are some which contrast considerably with each other. You could then discuss with the class ways in which two compositions might be combined so that a longer composition is produced. In doing so, you will need to think up, try out and discuss the effects of a wide range of possibilities. Take, for example two compositions, one of which is loud and the other is soft. These could be combined to produce the following types of pattern:

(a) Composition 1–loud	Composition 2–soft	Composition 1 repeated–loud
(b) Composition 1–loud	Composition 2–soft	Composition 1–shortened and played softly
(c) Composition 1	Composition 2	Elements of both compositions combined

These are just three of a very wide range of possibilities. As well as modifying the volume or shortening compositions, you could change the speeds or lengthen sections. By doing this, you will be giving the children the opportunity to keep searching for further variations to produce longer works and to focus increasingly on giving clear shape to their compositions.

Listen to the opening scene of Puccini's *La Boheme*. The students are in their garret and have no fuel to keep the fire going. In order to keep themselves warm, they burn the chair and finally the pages of a play which one of them has written. As the pages of the play go up in smoke, the students huddle round the fire pretending that they can see the action on the stage and offering comments on the quality of what has been written. Draw attention to the way that the orchestra is used to illustrate the fire flaring up, being rekindled or petering out. Having listened to this, encourage the children to reflect on how any ideas that they have heard in Puccini's work might be adapted and used to develop their own compositions.

58. RIGADON BY HENRY PURCELL

compositions quickly became very well known and, on his death at the very young age of 36, Purcell was described by one newspaper as 'one of the most celebrated Masters of the Science of Musick in the kingdom.'

Here is a song to a tune written by Purcell. The tune is known as 'rigadon' which is a type of dance which became very popular in Europe in Purcell's time.

Presentation
Teach the children to sing the tune and words of the song.

Starting note = G
Count in: 1 2 3 4 1 2 3 4

Rigadon

Come friends join the dance
Let's dance the night away
Come let's leap and prance
And let our masters pay
Rigadon rigadon don don don
Make fun and laughter
Rigadon rigadon don don don
Dance cares away

Purpose
To teach the children to sing and play a tune by Purcell and to add tuned and untuned percussion accompaniments to it; to introduce them to further examples of music by Purcell and enable them to begin to put it in a historical context; to introduce them to notes which are four beats in length.

Resources
Cassette: side 3, activity 58
Chime bars: G and D
Unpitched percussion instruments, e.g. claves and tambourine. These could be replaced by alternatives if necessary.
Copymaster 71

Background information
Henry Purcell was born in 1659 and lived at Westminster. Like his father before him, he became a musician at the royal court, first as a singer and then as a composer. He wrote music for voices, for instruments, for the church and for the theatre and was one of the first composers in England ever to write an opera. These

Start by teaching the children to sing the words and tune of the song along the lines suggested in the introduction to this book and using **Copymaster 71**. When they can perform this fairly confidently, practise saying the words and clapping out the rhythm of line 5:

Ri- ga-don	ri-ga don	don	don don Make
1	2	3	4	1	2	3	4
di -di da	di-di da	da	da da da

Do this over and over again in time to a steady beat. You can now divide the class into two groups: group 1 sings the tune, group 2 says and claps the rhythm in the above extract.

As the next stage, ask the children to clap out the rhythm of the words 'Fun and laughter' (line 6):

fun--------		and------		laugh-------ter----			
1	2	3	4	1	2	3	4
da	- a	da	- a	da	- a	da	- a
D		D		D		D	
G		G		G		G	

When the children can do this confidently divide them into three groups: group 1 sings the tune, group 2 says and claps the rhythm of 'Rigadon rigadon don don don make' and group 3 says and claps the rhythm of 'Fun and laughter'.

The next stage is to transfer the clapping to instruments. For this, group 2 could tap its rhythmic pattern on a tambourine while group 3 plays its rhythm on the chime bars G and D as indicated. To make sure that all children are singing and playing together, ask them to sing the words of their rhythms 'inside their heads'.

Now you are ready to rehearse a full performance. Try the following as a starter:

Count in 1 2 3 4 1 2 3 4 on claves and keep that beat going on the claves throughout.
Verse 1: voices and claves

Count in 1 2 3 4 1 2 3 4 adding the chime bars played by group 3.

Verse 2: Keep the chime bars and claves going throughout this verse

Count in 1 2 3 4 1 2 3 4 omitting the claves.
Verse 3: Keep the chime bars and tambourine going throughout the verse. In the last line slow the music down slightly.

End with a shake and a tap on the tambourine.

Extension
As a follow up to this activity, play the children sections of music by Purcell. The following are possible examples which you might wish to present to them.

- The Frost Scene from the opera *King Arthur*. This is famous for the way in which Purcell illustrates frost and cold through the shaking, trembling sound of the Cold Genius's voice.
- Dido's Lament from the opera *Dido and Aeneas*. Here draw their attention to the way that the lowest sounding instruments in the bass play the same music over and over again, even though the melody sung by the soprano changes and develops.

Come friends join the dance Let's dance the night a - way.

Come let's leap and prance And let our ma - sters pay.

Ri - ga- don ri - ga- don don don don Make fun and laugh - ter

Ri - ga- don ri - ga- don don don don Dance cares a - way.

59. THE COLD WINDS BLOW

Purpose

To introduce the children to ways of notating sounds which are four beats in length; to give them further experience of singing a song in canon and of adding pitched accompaniments to it.

Resources

Cassette: side 3, activity 59
Copymaster 72
Two sets of chime bars:
  Set 1: G and D
  Set 2: B and C

Presentation

Start by teaching the children the words and tune of the following Danish folk song.
Starting note: G
Count in: 1234

The Cold Winds Blow

The cold winds blow bringing ice and snow
To warmth of hearth and home we all gladly go.

When they can sing it confidently, ask them to march on the spot as they sing it. Then ask them to clap the rhythm as they march and sing. Alternatively, ask half the class to march and the other half to clap the rhythm. But all the children should sing. Now draw their attention to the length of the notes. Remind them that a sound which lasts for one beat = da, a sound which lasts for two beats = da-a, and a sound which lasts for three beats = da-a-a.

They should be able to identify the note lengths in the first bar very easily. Now sing the word 'blow' as they march on the spot. They will notice that this lasts for four beats. Explain that this is indicated with the syllable: da-a-a-a and the sign: O

Ask them to identify where else in this song there are notes which are four beats in length. (They appear, of course, on the words 'snow' and 'go'.)

Now ask the children to try beating out the patterns (in syllables and signs) at the top of **Copymaster 72**. As with other activities of this type, make sure that you have acquainted yourself thoroughly with this and practised the patterns before embarking on the activity with your class.

Extension 1

Taking the two sets of chime bars indicated above (one player per set) practise the following patterns.

Set 1		D		D		D		D
	G₁		G₁		G₁		G₁	
Set 2	B₁		C		B₁		B₁	
Count	1	2	3	4	1	2	3	4

When they can play it confidently, add this, as an accompaniment to the singers. They will need to play the pattern four times during one rendering of the tune.

Extension 2

This song can also be performed as a canon. It can be performed in 2, 3 or 4 parts. Each new voice enters as the previous one sings the syllable marked with an asterisk (*). Experiment to see in how many parts the class can sing the song comfortably. Do not move onto three parts if they cannot perform it in two parts.

When the children can perform the song as a canon, add the accompaniment. You could play the pattern outlined above through once before the first voice

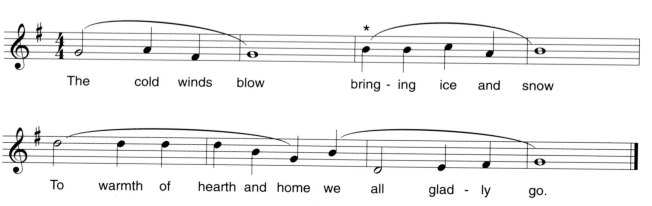

enters. With each voice involved in the canon, you will have to add one further rendering of the pattern. In addition to that, you could play one more version of the instrumental accompaniment pattern on its own after the last voice has finished.

As with other extension activities, the extent to which you can develop the work will depend very much on the abilities and experiences of the children with whom you are working.

60. AU CLAIRE DE LA LUNE

Purpose

To give the children further practice in performing, identifying and notating notes which are four beats in length; to give them further opportunities to see how melodies are given shape and form through the use of repeated melodic and rhythmic patterns.

Resources

Cassette: side 3, activity 60
Copymaster 73

Presentation

With the aid of the cassette **Copymaster 73** and the suggestions made in the introduction to this book, teach the children to sing the following song:

Starting note: G
Count in: 1 2 3 4

Au Clair de la Lune

Au claire de la lune mon ami Pierrot
Prete moi ta plume pour ecrire un mot
Ma chandelle est morte je n'ai plus de feu
Ouvre moi ta porte pour l'amour du Dieu.

When they can sing it fairly confidently, ask one half of the class to march regularly on the spot as they sing and the other half to clap out the rhythm of the notes as they sing. Then help the children identify which sounds extend for four beats. You will notice that they are the ones at the end of each line. From here, you can progress to showing the children that this melody has the same rhythmic pattern for every line, even when the melody changes. Help them also to hear that the tune has an AABA pattern, with the first, second and fourth lines having the same melody and a contrasting section in line 3. It is through the use of contrasts and similarities of this type that composers are able to produce variety in a tune without losing its sense of unity.

Next teach the children a further song involving four-beat notes. To identify these, adopt the same approach of marching and clapping that has already been described.

Starting note: B
Count in: 1 2 3 4

Now the Day is Over

Now the day is over, night is drawing nigh
Shadows of the evening steal across the sky.

Point out to the children that in this song the melody in the second half is different from that in the first half. But the rhythm is the same in both halves, so the melody retains its sense of unity. This melody has a pattern of A B.

61. THE SEASONS COMPOSITION

Purpose
To give children the opportunity to prepare, rehearse and present a performance of their own compositions to their peers and to other audiences within the school; to give them the opportunity to listen to Vivaldi's 'Seasons' and to identify and talk about the techniques composers adopt to convey a picture or mood through music; and to enable them to make decisions about how to construct a larger work by combining several shorter ones.

Resources
Four sets of instruments: each set should include a mixture of pitched and unpitched instruments.

Presentation
Involve the children in discussing the individual characteristics of the four seasons. They will probably take about the snow in winter, the leaves appearing on the trees and the arrival of lambs in the spring, the sunshine and holiday activities in the summer and the fall of the leaves in the autumn. Guide the discussion to an examination of the sounds and movements associated with each season. The following list might help you in prompting the discussion.

1. Spring sounds and movements: the high pitched bleating of lambs as opposed to the deeper sounding bleats of the ewes; the rapid movements of the lambs as they run around or shake their tails; the song of the birds as they build their nests; the flutter of new leaves in the trees.
2. Summer sounds and movements: here the children might choose to focus on sounds associated with holidays, e.g. a holiday at the seaside, in which case they might talk about the sound of children laughing, running along the sands, the movements of making holes in the sand; the rush of the waves, the sound of music from the pier.
3. Autumn sounds and movements: discussion here could focus on the movement of leaves as they fall; the swishing sound produced when you trudge through fallen leaves; the reduction in the number of birds and the fact that, as the days get colder and shorter, there are fewer people about and the world is quieter.
4. Winter sounds and movements: here the children might focus on the different types of movement of snow as it falls, sometimes very slowly and evenly, sometimes as a storm. They might talk about children shouting and laughing and having snowball fights or rushing down hillsides on sledges.

When they have had sufficient opportunity to discuss and record their ideas, divide the class into four groups, each to look further at a specific season of the year. If you have a large class, then arrange for the same season to be examined by more than one group. Assign a set of instruments to each group of children. Each set should include a mixture of pitched and unpitched percussion. Give each child a specific instrument, so that time is not wasted on chopping and changing instruments.

Now, using the techniques outlined on pages 13–16, ask each group to work on experimenting, presenting, discussing, drafting and redrafting a piece which can eventually be performed to the whole class. When the whole class is happy with each section, arrange for a performance of the four seasons to be presented. Where the class has been subdivided into several groups, you could have several performances of 'The Seasons'.

At this point, you might decide to record the performances. Alternatively, you could ask the class to decide which set of four seasons could be presented to the rest of the school or to parents at an assembly, for example. In making this decision, make sure that the pupils articulate their reasons and are able to identify the musical qualities and techniques which make a specific performance worth presenting. In this way, their critical skills will be developed. You might find that, after such discussion, the class might prefer to have a new combination of performances with the Autumn from group 1's work being combined with the Winter and Spring from group 2 and the Summer from group 3, for example.

In presenting the work to others, ask the children to make a short presentation, describing how they set about the task and what adaptations and developments they made. In this way, they will have the opportunity to reflect on the process as well as the product of their compositional work.

As a follow-up to this activity, play the children excerpts from Vivaldi's 'The Seasons'. After playing an excerpt a few times, encourage the children to comment not simply on what is being described in the music but how it is described and how effective they think it is. In doing this, they will be able to draw on and also extend their own awareness of the effects of combining sounds in particular ways. As with other music for listening, give the children the opportunity to return to it several times and to become familiar with it. A well-placed listening station in the classroom will be very useful for this purpose.

Background information
Vivaldi was an Italian composer, who was born in Venice in 1678. He was a very fine violinist and he composed a

vast amount of music. Many of these works were in the form of a concerto. This means that they were performed by one or two solo performers backed by a full orchestra. 'The Seasons' is a concerto written for a solo violinist and orchestra.

Many of Vivaldi's compositions were written when he was in charge of music at a famous school for girls in Venice. There were several of these in the city at the time. They had originally been set up as orphanages, but the teaching in them was so good and the musical talents of the pupils so great that soon girls came from all over Europe to be taught there. The women's orchestra at Vivaldi's school was particularly good and inspired some of his finest works.

62. MELODIC COMPOSITION

Purpose
To give the children the opportunity to apply their developing music-reading skills to sight reading a simple rhythmic pattern; to enable them to use the rhythmic pattern as a basis for creating their own melodies; to give them a basic understanding of what is meant by the term 'key' in music; to develop further their understanding of how repeated rhythmic and melodic patterns can be used to give shape to music.

Resources
Cassette: side 3, activity 62
Copymaster 74
Tambour or other unpitched percussion instrument
Chime bars: G A B C' D' E' F#' G'

Presentation
Start by reminding the children of the note values that they have already learnt:

| = one-beat note = da; ⊓ = two half-beat notes = di-di; ♩ = two-beat note = da-a; and ♩. = three-beat note = da-a-a.

Now help them to decipher the patterns on **Copymaster 74**. Start by asking them to identify which syllable should be applied to which symbol. Then, as you beat out a regular beat on a tambour or other unpitched percussion instrument, the children should say and clap the appropriate rhythmic pattern.

(I) | ⊓   ⊓ | | |
        da   di-di   di-di   da   da   da
        G

        | ⊓   ⊓   ♩.
        da   di-di   di-di   da - a - a
                     A

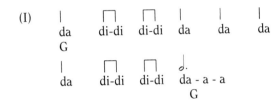

(I) | ⊓   ⊓ | | |
        da   di-di   di-di   da   da   da
        G

        | ⊓   ⊓   ♩.
        da   di-di   di-di   da - a - a
                     G

When they have done this and can clap the rhythm accurately, ask them to improvise a melody based on the rhythmic pattern. Ask them to make sure that the melody starts and finishes on the note G, that it reaches the note A half-way through and that the first and third lines are the same. Ask them to experiment with the arrangements several times before deciding on a particular order. Encourage them to aim for mainly step-wise movements but with some leaps to give variety. As with other compositional activities, give them the opportunity to present their developing ideas to each other for discussion, criticism and refinement along the lines suggested on pages 13–16.

When a child is satisfied with a particular version, ask him or her to write the names of the notes under the rhythmic indications on the copymaster so that they can remember the tune in future. You could also give the children the opportunity to play each other's melodies. This will ensure that they are applying the skills of reading and writing in a realistic context and as a means to an end rather than an end in themselves.

In addition to notating their tunes, the children could also record them on a cassette. In this way they can build up a 'folio' of their compositions.

Explain to the children that the arrangement of notes on the chime bars forms what is known as a scale of G major. The melodies which they have created are therefore said to be in G major.

63. BACH'S MINUET IN G

Purpose

To enable the children to listen to a minuet by Bach and to identify the way that repeated rhythmic patterns are used to give it shape; to give them some background information on Bach so that they can begin to put the music in a historical context; to give them the opportunity to listen to further examples of music by this composer.

Resources

Cassette: side 3, activity 63

Presentation

Remind the children of the explanation of the term G major and 'in G' introduced in Activity 62. Explain to them that they are going to hear a piece of music written in the scale of G major.

When they have listened to the melody a few times, draw the children's attention to the way that it makes use of a repeated rhythmic pattern which goes as follows:

| | ⊓ | ⊓ | | | | |
da   di-di   di-di   da   da   da

Help them to say and clap this pattern. They might well recognise it as the first line of the pattern already encountered in Activity 62. When they have familiarised themselves with it in this way, ask the children to listen for the rhythm as the melody is performed.

Background information

Johann Sebastian (J.S.) Bach was born in Germany in 1685. He was taught music by his father, himself a very well-known musician. Johann became a very fine organist and harpsichord player as well as a composer. As a young man, he worked as a composer and performer at the palaces of several princes before moving to the city of Leipzig, where he became organist and choir master at St Thomas's church. In this job, he had to compose a new work for the choir every week. He must have been very hard working as well as talented to be able to do all that. At Christmas time and other important festivals during the year, he had to write extra music to celebrate the event. On top of all this he had to teach Latin to the boys at the nearby school, a job which he hated, perhaps because the pupils would not listen to him and kept misbehaving.

Bach was married twice and had 21 children in all. The minuet which you have just heard and played was specially written by Bach for his second wife, Anna Magdalena, when he was teaching her to play the harpsichord. It is still a popular piece for teaching people today and many people learning to play the piano will have played it.

During his lifetime, Bach wrote a vast amount of music for choirs, the organ, the harpsichord and also for orchestras. When he died in 1750, however, his music was soon forgotten and was not again made famous until a hundred years later when another German composer, Felix Mendelssohn, rediscovered his music and set about making it well known to people again. Today J.S. Bach is one of the most famous names in the world of music.

Listening

Play the children excerpts from Bach's music. The following are possibilities: Toccata and Fugue in D Minor for organ; one of the Brandenburg Concertos.

81

64. THE HARPSICHORD

Purpose

To give the children the experience of listening to music played on the harpsichord and piano; to enable them to identify and differentiate between these instruments when they are being played; to give them an elementary notion of how the sounds of the harpsichord are produced and how they differ in their mechanism and sound from the piano.

Resources

Cassette: side 4, activity 64
Copymaster 75

Presentation

Remind the children of the work pursued in Activity 63. Explain to them that the instrument on which they heard Bach's 'Minuet in G' being performed was a harpsichord. This keyboard instrument was very popular from the sixteenth to the eighteenth centuries, before the invention of the piano. When a player presses one of the keys on the harpsichord, the strings inside are plucked. This is different from the piano where the pressing of a key causes a hammer inside to hit the strings.

On the piano, the harder you hit the key, the louder the sound. In the case of the harpsichord, however, you cannot produce variations of volume by changing the pressure. Instead, harpsichords often have two sets of keyboards, one of which plays more loudly than the other. The performer produces contrasts of volume by moving from one keyboard (or 'manual') to the other. Each manual can be set at a particular volume by drawing out stops. When some stops are out they cause more than one note to play as the performer presses one key. This makes the sound louder. Now ask them to complete the listening puzzle on Copymaster 75. The answers are as follows: (1) Harpsichord (2) Piano (3) Piano (4) Harpsichord (5) Harpsichord.

65. FIREWORKS COMPOSITION PROJECT

Purpose

To give the children further experience of creating their own compositions using visual and aural stimuli; to enable them to notate their compositions and decipher others' notations; and to give them further experience of preparing and presenting performances of their own and each others' compositions.

Resources

A range of pitched and unpitched instruments
Copymaster 76

Presentation

Start by talking to the children about fireworks displays they might have attended. Guide the conversation to a discussion of the various types of fireworks they have seen. Some fireworks make very sudden bangs. Others make a whooshing sound and then a loud bang. Some fireworks make a tremendous crackling noise while others make very little noise but change colours as they burn. Rockets, of course, make a whooshing sound as

they rise upwards. In some cases that is the end of the matter but some rockets then descend in a series of loud explosions. Catherine wheels spin round while other types jump along the ground. These are just a few examples but they should be sufficient to prompt discussion and the children will no doubt be able to describe many more types.

Encourage them to concentrate on the sounds produced: on whether the sound occurs suddenly or builds up gradually, on how loud it is and also on how quickly or slowly the firework and its sound die away.

When they have had sufficient time to talk, ask the children individually to think of a specific type of firework. Then, in pairs and with instruments of their own choice, ask them to produce a sound which will illustrate it.

The following suggestions could be used to prompt some children. A rocket could be illustrated by a quick strike on a rasp followed by a flurry of notes on the chime bar to illustrate the stars falling from it in the sky. A crackling firework could be illustrated with several rasps and other unpitched wooden percussion instruments while a firework that changes colour could be represented by a change of instruments and tone colour.

When they have had time to experiment, practise and arrive at a preliminary idea, ask each pair to perform to the rest of the class for comment and further ideas for development.

Now arrange the children into groups of six or eight. Each group's task will be to put the fireworks sounds together into a display. Before doing so, discuss with the children what they have noticed at displays. Quite often, groups of similar fireworks will be set off within a short time of each other so that you might have several rockets going off in quick succession followed by crackling fireworks on the ground. Just as these are beginning to peter out, a set of quieter fireworks might be seen changing colour before another louder series of fireworks is set off. This gives variety and contrast to the visual display. They must try to produce similar variety and contrast in their compositions.

As suggested in the introduction (pp. 13–16), give the children the opportunity to practise, to perform emerging ideas to each other, to comment on their own and each other's work and to redraft the ideas. When each group is happy with the effects produced, arrange a performance of the music to the rest of the class or to other members of the school.

As a development of this you could ask the children, when they are producing their pieces, to make pictures of the sounds produced and the way that they are put together, concentrating on trying to make a visual representation of the sound. Thus a loud sound might be more heavily coloured or have thicker lines. Pitch can of course be indicated by differing heights on the paper. These scores should be as colourful as possible and could, in themselves, be an attractive addition to the classroom display. They could also be transferred between groups so that children have to interpret each others' notations.

A further activity could be to present the pupils with the firework symbols in **Copymaster 76** and ask them to build a composition based on this. They could experiment with the sounds first and then arrange the symbols accordingly. Alternatively, they could simply arrange the visual patterns and then practise interpreting and performing them. As with other compositions, they could tape their final versions.

Listening

George Friedrich Handel was born in 1685, the same year as J.S. Bach. Handel worked as composer and musician at the courts of various dukes and princes, and travelled extensively to Italy and Britain. In 1749 in London he composed some music to accompany a firework display and this music is still popular today.

Play the excerpt from the 'Royal Fireworks music'. Explain to the children that the music was originally to be played by wind instruments only but later stringed instruments were added. Ask the children to try to identify the wind instruments which they hear. Also draw their attention to the use of the kettle drums or timpani. For the first performance, Handel borrowed the army's kettle drums from the Tower of London.

66. THE EMPEROR'S HYMN – HAYDN

Purpose

To teach the children to sing the 'Emperor's Hymn' by Haydn and to add a simple bass accompaniment to it; to introduce them to the nature and sound of a string quartet.

Resources

Cassette: side 4, activity 66
Chime bars: D E G A
Copymaster 77

Background information

Joseph Haydn was born in Austria in 1732. He was a very musical boy and he loved to listen to the band when it practised or marched through the town. But what he wanted to do most of all was to play with them. He didn't want to play the trumpet or the glockenspiel or one of the wind instruments; what he desperately wanted to play was the biggest instrument of all – the big bass drum. But whenever he told anybody this they would just laugh and tell him not to be so silly. The instrument was far too big for a little child. He could not even lift it up, let alone carry it or play it in a procession.

But there was one man who lived in the town who did not laugh at Joseph. This man knew all too well how painful it could be when people laughed at you. When he had been a small boy himself, he had had a very serious illness which had left him with a very bent back so that he could never stand up straight. People used to be very cruel and laugh at him because of this. What they did not realise was what a kind and sensitive man he was. When he saw how upset little Joseph was, he felt very sorry for him. 'But it's no use just being sorry for him. I must try to help him', he said to himself. And that's when he had a brilliant idea. Next time he saw Joseph and his aunt in the town, he told them what his idea was. The surprise would come a few weeks later when there was a holiday and there would be a fair and other celebrations in the town square.

The great day dawned. Then came the big moment when the mayor of the town appeared wearing his fine robes and chain of office. He took his place on a special stand outside the town hall ready to judge the fancy dress competition which was a very popular part of the festivities. All the competitors would march into the town square, past the mayor, who would then decide who deserved the prize for the best costume. Down the street they came in a great procession, headed by the town band. In the middle of this column was an amazing sight. The old man with the crooked back was walking and strapped to his back was the bass drum. Immediately behind was the little five-year-old Joseph Haydn hitting the drum with a huge drum stick and keeping the march in order. A great cheer went up and everyone said that the band had never marched so well as on that day because no one had ever kept the beat so regularly as young Joseph Haydn.

It did not come as a surprise to the people of Hainburg when, in later years, Joseph Haydn became one of the most famous composers in Europe. They remembered that day when the band marched better than it had ever marched before or since.

Presentation

Explain to the children that one of the most famous tunes written by Haydn was 'The Emperor's Hymn'. During a visit to England, Haydn heard and admired the British national anthem. He was so impressed by this

that, when he got back home, he decided to write a similar anthem. This was dedicated to the Austrian Emperor who was so delighted with it that he gave Haydn a gold box with an engraving of the emperor's head on it. It is still the national anthem of Austria today and, in Britain, the tune is used for a famous hymn, 'Glorious Things of Thee are Spoken'.

Now teach the children to sing the hymn.

Starting note = D
Count in: 1 2 3 4 1 2 3 4

The Emperor's Hymn

Glorious things of thee are spoken
Zion city of our God
He whose word cannot be broken
Form'd thee for his own abode
On the Rock of Ages founded
What can shake thy sure repose?
With salvation's walls surrounded
Thou may'st smile on all thy foes.

When the children can sing the melody with confidence, try adding the chime bar accompaniment indicated on the **Copymaster 7**. You might wish to do this yourself or ask one of the children to do so.

Listening

From here you can progress to explaining to the children that Haydn used this tune in his 'Emperor' string quartet. Play them an excerpt from that work. Explain to them that a string quartet is a piece written for four instruments – usually two violins, a viola and a cello. The tune appears in the second movement of the string quartet.

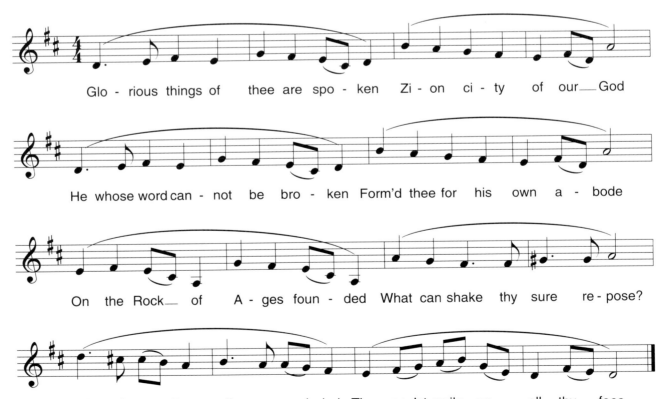

67. THE STRING QUARTET

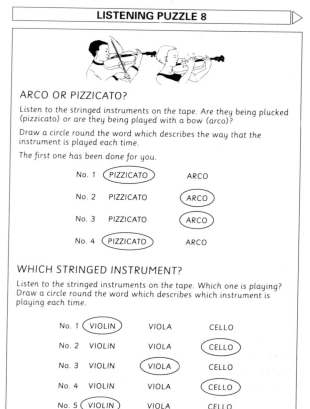

ARCO OR PIZZICATO?

Listen to the stringed instruments on the tape. Are they being plucked (pizzicato) or are they being played with a bow (arco)?

Draw a circle round the word which describes the way that the instrument is played each time.

The first one has been done for you.

No. 1	(PIZZICATO)	ARCO
No. 2	PIZZICATO	(ARCO)
No. 3	PIZZICATO	(ARCO)
No. 4	(PIZZICATO)	ARCO

WHICH STRINGED INSTRUMENT?

Listen to the stringed instruments on the tape. Which one is playing? Draw a circle round the word which describes which instrument is playing each time.

No. 1	(VIOLIN)	VIOLA	CELLO
No. 2	VIOLIN	VIOLA	(CELLO)
No. 3	VIOLIN	(VIOLA)	CELLO
No. 4	VIOLIN	VIOLA	(CELLO)
No. 5	(VIOLIN)	VIOLA	CELLO

Purpose

To give the children the opportunity to listen to the instruments which make up a string quartet; to identify their sounds individually and in combination; and to differentiate between them.

Resources

Cassette: side 4, activity 67
Copymasters 78 and 79

Presentation

Using **Copymaster 78**, explain to the children the basic principles of sound production on a stringed instrument and how such instruments can be plucked ('pizzicato') or bowed ('arco'). Play the first set of extracts on the cassette to illustrate this. When they have listened to this, ask them to listen to the next part of the track to identify how the sounds are played. They should enter their answers on **Copymaster 79**. The answers are opposite.

Explain to the children that, as with other instruments, the larger the instrument the lower the range of

sounds it will produce. Thus the highest sounds are produced by the violin. Play them the examples of violin sounds on the cassette. In a string quartet, there are usually two violins. The lowest sounds in a string quartet are produced by the cello, and the middle range of sounds by the viola. All of these instruments can be heard on the cassette.

Let the children listen to these examples several times, in order to familiarise themselves with the various sounds. When they have sufficient practice at this, ask them to identify which instrument is playing by filling in the second puzzle on Copymaster 79. The answers to the questions are as above.

68. VARIATIONS

Purpose

To give the children experience of listening to a theme and variations; to identify and discuss what techniques the composer uses to produce variety; to introduce them to the terms 'legato' and 'staccato'.

Resources

Cassette: side 4, activity 68

Before embarking on this activity, you might find it useful to remind the children of what they have already learnt in Activities 19, 22 & 25.

Presentation:

Start by asking the children to sing the tune of 'Happy Birthday'. Then explain to them that they are going to listen to this tune being played on the piano. It will be played through once followed by four variations. They must listen very carefully and try to work out how the tune has been varied. Play the piece through to them several times so that they can get to know it and comment on it. Then involve them in discussing the techniques used. The features which they might be able to identify for themselves, or to which you can help guide their attention, are as follows. First, the tune is played through fairly softly (mezzo piano). In variation 1, the tune is broken up so that sections of accompaniment are heard in between. This time the music is played loudly (forte). In variation 2, the pitch range is very high and the notes are quick (allegro) and detached (staccato). In variation 3, the music is very soft (pianissimo) and smooth (legato). In variation 4, the music is slow (largo) and loud (forte).

(It is not essential for the children to use the Italian terms. What is most important is that they can describe accurately what they hear. However, you need to be sure that, if they do apply Italian terms, they do so correctly. This will be easier if you have pursued the revision work suggested above.)

69. THE ORCHESTRA

Purpose

To introduce the children to the make up of the symphony orchestra and to acquaint them further with its sound.

Resources

Copymaster 80

Presentation:

Start by reminding the children of the work already pursued on the string quartet. A string quartet, they will remember, consists of two violins, viola and cello. In an orchestra you will again find these instruments but this time in far greater numbers. There are two groups of violinists, known as the first violin and second violin sections, groups of viola players and groups of cellists. In addition, an orchestra also contains a small number of double basses, the largest and deepest of the string instruments. Together, these instruments form the string section of the orchestra.

In addition to the strings there are three other sections: the brass section which includes instruments such as trumpets, horns and trombones; the woodwind section which includes piccolos, flutes, clarinets and bassoons; and the percussion section made up of such instruments as drums, triangles, cymbals and glockenspiels.

The children have already encountered several of these instruments at an earlier point. To help remind them, you might need to revise the work done in Activities 44, 45, 53 and 54.

The precise size and composition of the orchestra has varied from one period of musical history to another and also from one composition to another. Some composers have made use of fairly small orchestras while others have demanded very large resources.

To complete the 'I-spy in the concert hall' activity on the copymaster, arrange for the children to visit a concert hall or, if that is not feasible, let them see a video of an orchestra in action. It is important that this activity is brought to life in this way. Many orchestras and opera companies now have education officers who will provide you with further information and help arrange projects where the children can meet orchestral performers and join with them in composition and performing activities. These projects are often arranged to take place in the school. A directory such as *The British Music Education Year Book* will give you details of whom to contact. Your local library should also be able to refer you to other helpful directories.

Listening

Play some examples of orchestral music, e.g. any symphony by Haydn or Mozart, any symphony by Brahms or Tchaikovsky: Stravinsky's *Rite of Spring* or one of Mahler's symphonies.

70. THE SURPRISE

Purpose

To extend the children's acquaintance with the music of Haydn and to give them further experience of listening to a symphony orchestra.

Resources

Recording of Haydn's 'Surprise' symphony

Background information

Remind the children of the work already pursued on the music of Haydn in Activity 72. Then go on to explain that Haydn spent most of his working life at the court of one of the richest noblemen in Europe, the Prince of Esterhazy. There he had to compose music, teach singing and rehearse and conduct the orchestra.

After Prince Anton, his employer, died, Haydn was invited to visit England and give concerts there. He wrote several new symphonies to be performed during his visit. These were well received and soon Haydn became very popular with the London audiences.

In London, however, Haydn noticed that before coming to the concerts, people would often have a very

heavy meal which made some of them rather sleepy. Although they could usually keep awake during the loud, fast, first movement of a symphony, many of them fell fast asleep during the soft, slow movement.

Haydn decided to play a trick on such people. The second movement of his next symphony was again slow and relaxing and several members of the audience began to nod off. But, just as they did so, Haydn had written into the score a very loud chord. Any sleepers must have jumped out of their skin and cannot have been so ready to go off to sleep again so rudely.

This symphony is still very popular today and, because of what happens in the second movement, is known as the 'Surprise' symphony. Try listening to it. And remember: Don't go to sleep!

Presentation

Play the children an extract from the second movement of Haydn's Symphony No. 94 in G Major, the 'Surprise'. Draw their attention to the use which the composer makes of sudden loud chords in this music.

71. MINUET IN F

Purpose

To introduce the children to the music of Mozart by listening to extracts from his compositions and by performing an arrangement of one of his pieces; to give the children the opportunity to play a simple tune with bass accompaniment; to give them further practice in listening to a melody and discussing the pattern on which it is based; to enable them to identify and discuss the differences between an original version of a piece of music and an arrangement of it.

Resources

Cassette: side 4, activity 71
Copymaster 81
Chime bars: F G A B♭ C' D' E' F'
Bass xylophone or bass metallophone notes: C₁ F₁ A₁ B♭₁ C arranged as indicated in Copymaster 81. (If these instruments are not available, use additional chime bars or the piano. If the latter is used, you will need the piano chart from **Copymasters 37–38**. You might also need to remind the children and yourself of how to use this by referring back to Activity 35.

Presentation:

Start by playing the recording of the arrangement of Minuet in F on the cassette. Do this several times, to familiarise the children with the piece and to give them a notion of the type of sound they should be aiming to produce.

As they listen to the music, ask the children to tap the beat gently, putting a slight accent on the beat marked 1 each time. Now focus their attention on the bass line at the top of the copymaster. Start by helping them to decipher the rhythm, using the syllables learnt in earlier activities. Remind them that | = da = one-beat note, ⊓ = di-di = two half-beat notes, ♩ = da-a = two-beat note and ♩. = da-a-a = three-beat note.

Starting note: F
Count in: 1 2 3

When the children have deciphered the rhythmic notation on the copymaster and can clap it, ask them to clap it with the cassette. From here you can progress to teaching them to play the notes. The most confident can

then play this accompaniment while the others clap the rhythm. This section of the work will take time and practice, so do not expect it all to be mastered in one lesson.

The next stage is to teach the children to decipher the rhythm of the melody. Start by asking them to listen to the cassette again, this time focusing specifically on the melody and its rhythmic pattern. When they have done this, help them to decipher the rhythm, again using the syllables learnt earlier. The rhythm of the melody is shown at the bottom of the copymaster.

Draw the children's attention to the way that the melody makes considerable use of repeated rhythmic patterns. When the children have mastered this, try playing the melody. You could do this by asking one child to play the whole tune. Alternatively, one child could practise line 1, while a second child practises line 2. (You will need to have two sets of chime bars if you do this.) To perform the whole melody, the first player would play line 1, the second player would play line 2, then the first player would play the final two lines which are repeats of the first two lines. When the children can play this fairly confidently, let them play it along with the cassette.

Draw their attention to the fact that, although the third line has the same rhythm and melody as lines 1 and 4, the accompanying notes change, thus giving it a different character. This is another way in which a composer can give unity to a tune by repeating some features while, at the same time, giving it variety by changing other features slightly.

When this has been done, try adding the accompaniment to the tune. It must be re-emphasised that this activity needs time. Precisely how much you can achieve will depend on the children's experiences and abilities. Even if they cannot tackle all the performance aspects, make sure that all the children are involved in deciphering and performing the rhythms and also in listening to and analysing the way that the melody has been constructed.

When this has been done, explain to the children that what they have been playing is an arrangement of a small extract from the minuet as it was written by Mozart. To emphasise this, play the complete version on the cassette, and discuss with the children how the original version differs from the arrangement. The points which they might identify or to which you could draw their attention are that:

● the original version is longer and is played on a harpsichord;
● the bass line involves a wider range of notes and greater rhythmic variety;
● there is a pause towards the end of the original version;
● in the middle section of the original version, the music changes its mood and character;
● in the first line of the melody of the original version, there is more rhythmic variety than in the arrangement.

Extension
Explain to the children that Mozart was an Austrian composer who lived from 1756 to 1791; that he was a child prodigy; that the minuet they have just heard was composed when he was only 6 and that Mozart's music is very widely performed. Ask them to find more information about him and make this the basis of a display. You could also ask them to identify how many of his works are being broadcast during the time that you are pursuing this activity and arrange for the children to listen to such a broadcast.

72. ODE TO JOY

Purpose
To introduce the children to the music of Beethoven through performing and listening to extracts from his works.

Resources
Cassette: side 4, activity 72
Copymaster 82

Background information
During the Second World War, people in countries occupied by the Germans were forbidden to listen to the BBC. Despite the dangers, many did so. Even when there were no programmes being broadcast, the BBC broadcast a drum rhythm which became known to people all over the continent. The rhythm went like this:

di di di da-a-a

Listen to it on the cassette and then try playing it yourself. In Morse Code, the pattern ... — represents

89

the letter V for Victory. Those listening to the BBC in the 1940s knew that this code was meant to give them hope of eventual victory. It is interesting that this rhythm was taken from the work of a composer who was in fact German: Ludwig van Beethoven. Beethoven builds the whole of the first movement of his Fifth Symphony around that rhythm. Listen to the first part of movement 1 of Beethoven's Fifth Symphony and try to work out how often this rhythm is played.

Ludwig van Beethoven was born in Bonn, Germany in 1770 but spent most of his life in Vienna, Austria, where he died in 1828. He wrote a vast amount of music for the piano, as well as string quartets, symphonies, church music and an opera; and all this despite the fact that for a large part of his life he was totally deaf. In all, Beethoven wrote nine symphonies. Up until his time, symphonies were pieces for instruments only, but Beethoven's Ninth Symphony includes a choir of voices as well as instruments. In the last movement of the symphony, the choir sings a tune which has become very famous and is known as 'Ode To Joy'. This tune is now the anthem of the European Community. So, not only has Beethoven's music been used to symbolise hope during the dark days of war, it is also now being used to celebrate the peace that exists between the countries concerned.

Presentation
Teach the children this version of the 'Ode To Joy', using **Copymaster 82** and the music below.

Starting note: F#
Count in: 1 2 3 4 1 2 3 4

Ode to Joy

Praise to Joy the God descended
Daughter of Elysium
Ray of mirth and rapture blended
Goddess to they shrine we come
By thy magic is united
What stern Custom parted wide
All mankind are brothers plighted
Where thy gentle wings abide.

Encourage the children to sing with a strong, confident sound to convey the spirit of the words. When they have practised and performed the 'Ode to Joy' play them an extract from the last movement of the Ninth Symphony so that they can hear how the tune sounds in its original context.

Extension
As with the work on Mozart (Activity 71), you could involve the children in discovering more about Beethoven and listing the works which they have heard on the radio, television or in any other context.

90

73. SCHUBERT SONG

Purpose

To introduce the children to the music of Schubert and to enable them to begin to place it in a historical context; to extend the children's listening skills by focusing their attention on musical devices used to convey a 'picture' through music; to enable the children to apply previous experiences to the identification of instruments used within an orchestral texture; to extend their experience of vocal music and their abilities to differentiate between various vocal timbres.

Resources

Cassette: side 4, activity 73
Copymaster 83

Background information

Franz Schubert was born in Vienna in 1797 and died there in 1828. He was always brimming with ideas for new compositions and sometimes, when a new idea seized him, he forgot about others on which he was already working. As a result, quite a few of his compositions were never finished.

Schubert was one of a group of musicians, artists and writers who lived in Vienna. There is a story that, on one occasion, when Schubert and a group of his friends visited a coffee shop together, Schubert was seized with the urge to compose. The friends called for the bill and began to get ready to leave. However, Schubert started to mutter to himself and his eyes began to dart around the room. As soon as he caught sight of the inkwell and quill on the counter, he got up out of his seat and helped himself to it. 'Paper, paper,' he muttered to himself as he began to look around again feverishly. Before anyone could stop him, he went over to an empty table and began to draw lines in ink on the fresh, clean tablecloth. Then, as quick as a flash, he covered the lines with notes of music. All this time his friends were cheering him on. 'It's my very best one yet,' said Franz. 'Come on, I'll sing it to you'. And without a by-your-leave he dragged the

tablecloth off the table and rushed off to his house with his friends laughing and joking behind him.

Presentation

As well as writing for full orchestra, Schubert also composed music for other groups of instruments and for the piano. But it is for his songs that he is best remembered. One of the best loved of these is the following lullaby. Using the cassette, **Copymaster 83** and the suggestions in the introduction to this book, teach the lullaby to the children.

Starting note: D
Count in: 1 2 3 (NB The first word is sung on beat 4)

Lullaby

Hush, sweet.
Gently sleep.
Shades of night are falling,
Calling you away
From the cares of day.
Angels high above
Guard you with their love
Hush, sweet.
Gently sleep.
Sleep till morning light returns.

When the children have learnt the words and the tune and can sing them fairly confidently, work on ensuring that each phrase of the music is sung smoothly, that the volume is soft and that the atmosphere of a lullaby is captured in the performance.

Explain to the children that in this song the piano accompaniment supports the melody and moves very much with the voice. In many of Schubert's songs, however, the piano has a very independent part to play and is used to create a 'musical picture' around the words. Play the children the second musical extract on this track. When they have heard it once, explain to them that the song describes an old man standing at the end of a street on a freezing cold day. He is playing a barrel-organ and is busking in order to get enough money to feed himself. His fingers are stiff and cold and, in the cap at his feet, there is very little money.

Having told them this, ask the children to listen to the song again and to focus on how Schubert 'paints' this picture through his music. Among the points that the children might identify for themselves, or to which you could draw their attention, are the following.

- The music is soft and slow to give the impression of the muffled sound effects of a cold, snowy day in winter.
- When the voice sings, it usually does so with very little accompaniment. This gives the impression of the loneliness of the old man as he plays on, ignored by the passers by.
- The pianist plays the same two notes in the left hand. This gives the impression of the low, drone sound that is heard when a hurdy-gurdy is played.
- In the right hand of the piano (the higher pitched notes), a short snippet of a melody is heard. This starts a

flurry of quick notes which then slow into longer ones. This gives the impression of the way the old man is too tired or old to be able to keep the handle of the hurdy-gurdy moving at a regular speed.

When the children have discussed and identified such features, play it to them again, so that they extend their reaction to the music by drawing on added insights. In this type of work remember to focus not so much on what picture is being conveyed by the music but on *how* it is conveyed.

Hush, sweet. Gen - tly sleep. Shades of night are fa - lling.

Ca - lling you a - way, From the cares of day.

An - gels high a - bove, Guard you with their love.

Hush, sweet. Gen - tly sleep. Sleep till mor - ning light re - turns.

74. ROBERT AND CLARA SCHUMANN

Purpose
To introduce the children to the music of Robert and Clara Schumann; to enable them to identify stepwise movement in a melody; to identify repeated phrases and gradations of volume; to identify how accompanimental figures can give a particular mood or character to a melody.

Resources
Cassette: side 4, activity 74

Background information
Robert Schumann was a German composer who lived from 1810 to 1856. Originally he intended to become a lawyer but eventually became a concert pianist. Any pianist will tell you that the weakest finger, and the one which causes most difficulty when performing, is the fourth finger on the left hand. Robert realised this and decided to strengthen it using a special machine which he devised involving weights which had to be lifted by that finger. Unfortunately, the only effect this contraption had on Schumann was to damage his finger beyond repair, so that he could no longer continue his career as a pianist. Instead, he turned his attention to composing and, during his short life, produced large numbers of songs and pieces for the piano as well as symphonies and other orchestral works.

Presentation

Start by listening to Schumann's 'A Little Piece'. When the children have listened to the piece once or twice to familiarise themselves with it, ask them to listen to it again, this time concentrating on the way that the melody sounds. Through questions and discussion, guide their attention to the following features of the music.

• The way that the melody in the right hand (the highest sounding notes) moves very smoothly, making considerable use of stepwise movement from one note to the next.

• The way that in the left hand there is a similar melody which echoes that in the right hand; the way that the melody in the right hand makes use of only two types of notes: one-beat notes (da) and two-beat notes (da-a), while in the left hand there are half-beat notes (di-di) all the way through. This left-hand accompaniment adds to the flowing nature of the music. To reinforce this, ask the children to clap out the rhythm of the first right-hand phrase:

```
          da   da        da   da   da   da
          |    |         |    |    |    |
   1   2  3    4      1   2    3    4
  da - a     da   da      da   da   da   da
   𝅗𝅥          |    |       |    |    |    |
   1   2    3    4       1   2    3    4
  da   da
   |    |
   1    2
```

• The way that the music starts softly (piano), builds up (through a crescendo), becomes piano again, builds up through a second crescendo and then returns to piano at the end.

In 'A Little Piece', the smooth flow of the melody is

supported by the way that the left-hand accompaniment moves in regular half-beats.

Now ask the children to listen to the second extract on the track: where the left hand produces a very different effect. This is another piano piece by Robert Schumann in which he describes a horseman riding by. When they have heard it a few times, to familiarise them with it, ask them the following questions.

1. How does the composer give the impression that the horse is galloping? (Through the use of a repeated jagged rhythm in the lower pitched notes. This sounds like the rhythm that a horse's hooves produce when it is galloping.)

2. How does the composer give the impression that the horse is passing by? (He does so through the use of gradations of volume. The music starts very softly – pianissimo – builds up to fortissimo – very loud – half-way through and there is a reduction in volume – diminuendo – until finally the music is pianissimo again.)

To help the children with this work, it will be useful to revise the work on Italian terms encountered earlier in the book (e.g. Activities 19, 22 & 25).

From here you can go on to explain to the children that, when Robert Schumann decided to become a concert pianist, he took lessons from a very fine teacher called Friedrick Wieck. Wieck had a brilliant daughter called Clara who had made a reputation for herself as a virtuoso pianist and composer when she was still a very young girl. Clara and Robert fell in love and wanted to marry but Friedrick opposed this. Eventually Clara took her father to court and the couple were given permission to marry.

Clara continued her performing and composing career after her marriage as well as running a home and bringing up several children. For a long time, her compositions were forgotten but now they are happily enjoying a revival.

75. BRAHMS

(For each set, you will need two players: one to play the lowest note, the other to play the remaining two notes)
Copymasters 84 and 85.

Presentation

Start by reminding the children of the work already done, in the preceding activity, on the music of Robert and Clara Schumann. Explain that a close friend of the Schumann's was the composer Johannes Brahms who wrote the next piece of music that they are going to perform. Introduce this section of the activity by teaching the children to sing the words and the tune of Brahms's 'Lullaby':

Starting note: E
Count in: 1 2 3 1 2 (NB The first word is sung on the third beat)

Purpose

To introduce the children to the music of Brahms and to enable them to begin to put it in a historical context; to teach them to sing Brahms's 'Lullaby' and to enable them to add a simple chordal accompaniment to it.

Resources

Cassette: side 4, activity 75
Three sets of chime bars:
  Set 1: C E G
  Set 2: G, B, D
  Set 3: F, A, C

Lullaby

Hush my dear one, Goodnight
May the stars shine their light
May heavenly moonbeams shed
Silver haloes round your head
May the angels above guard you with their love
Sleep till night is cast away and we welcome back
  the day

As with the Schubert Lullaby in Activity 73, make sure that the children sing the tune smoothly and softly

94

and that each full phrase is sung to one breath. When they can do this fairly confidently, ask them to mark the beat as they sing. They could start by tapping each beat gently on their laps. Later, they tap the beats marked 1 and clap the other two with claps. Bear in mind that this is a lullaby and therefore the movements should not be allowed to become too vigorous or the first beats too accented. The instrumentalists could now practise adding their part, as shown on **Copymaster 84**. Start by asking both children in each group to play on the first beat. Then progress to the point where the first child plays on the first beat and the second child plays on beats 2 and 3. As with previous activities of this type, give the children time to practise. Also remember to ask the children to sing, even when they are playing the instruments, so that the synchronisation is maintained. When all are performing together, make sure that they listen to each other and that the accompaniment is not allowed to drown the sound of the singing.

When they have completed these activities, explain to the children that the song which they have just learnt was written by the composer Johannes Brahms. Brahms was born in Hamburg, Germany, in 1833 and died in Vienna in 1897. He composed many works, including songs, symphonies and piano music. He first came to fame when the composer Robert Schumann wrote newspaper articles praising his work. Towards the end of his life, the University of Breslau awarded him the degree of Doctor of Music. To celebrate that occasion, Brahms wrote a work for orchestra called 'The Academic Festival Overture' in which he included several favourite student songs. Among them was 'Gaudeamus

Igitur', a German student song which was originally sung in Latin.

With the aid of the cassette **Copymaster 85** and the suggestions included in the introduction to this book, teach the children the following song.

Starting note: F
Count in: 1 2 3

Gaudeamus Igitur

Come my friends let's sing and shout
Fun is what our life's about
Soon all this will pass you'll see,
So come on let's make merry
Briefly lasts all joy and laughter
Pain and suffering soon come after
Then into the ground we pass
And our lives are o'er alas!

Make sure that the children perform this song with gusto, producing a loud, confident tone but without degenerating into shouting.

Listening
When they have learnt the song, play them the 'The Academic Festival Overture' by Brahms.

Extension
As with other activities of this type, you could follow it up with a 'research' activity where the children discover more about the composer and listen to other examples of his work on records or through broadcasts.

95

76. SLEEP COMPOSITION

Purpose

To give the children further experience of composing, using a particular mood, volume and tempo as a starting point.

Resources

Several sets of four to five instruments. Each set should include a mixture of pitched and unpitched percussion instruments.

Presentation

Remind the children of the lullabies sung in the two preceding activities. Discuss with them the characteristics which were common to both. They will probably mention – or you could guide their attention to – such features as:

- the moderately slow pace of the music;
- the soft volume;
- the smooth flowing phrases.

Explain to the children that they are not going to compose a lullaby as such. Instead they are going to produce pieces which describe the various stages of going to sleep. One example is given here.

1st Stage: The person is wide awake but decides to sit down. How would this be reflected in volume and speed? (The person would become a little quieter and would slow down. Because the person is making a large movement, from a standing to a sitting position, the overall effect might be reflected in the use of most or all of the instruments.)

2nd Stage: The person is sitting calmly. How could this be reflected in music? (Possible through a moderately soft melodic idea.)

3rd Stage: The person begins to nod off. (This might be reflected through a slowing down and softening of the melody. The music might also be interspersed with irregular silences.)

4th Stage: The person sleeps. (A new very soft melody might now be introduced. Occasionally, this could be interspersed with louder sounds as the person starts and momentarily opens his or her eyes.)

5th Stage: The person slips off into a deep sleep. (Here the music might get softer and softer and slower and slower until eventually it disappears entirely.)

If such a structure were devised in discussion, you could then adopt a variety of approaches to turning it into a composition. You might choose five groups, each of which would work on a different section. The sections would then be brought together at the end into a complete composition which could be recorded. An alternative approach would be to focus on the production of two melodies, stages 2 and 4. These could be played in their entirety in those sections but fragments of them could also be used in the other sections. In this way, the work of the separate groups could be welded more successfully into one piece.

An alternative approach might be to ask one group to create each section. These are just two of myriad possibilities. Experiment with various approaches and decide on the one(s) best suited to the particular class and conditions in which you are working.

77. MAJOR AND MINOR

sounding version – is said to be in a major key while the sadder, second version is said to be in a minor key.

Explain to them that most of the tunes which they have performed hitherto have been in major scales but they are now going to learn a song in a minor key. This is a Jewish song of farewell, 'Shalom Chaverim'.

Using the cassette **Copymaster 86** and the suggestions in the introduction to this book, teach the children to sing this song.

Starting note: B
Count in: 1 2 3 4 1 2 3 (NB The first syllable is sung on the fourth beat of the bar).

Shalom Chaverim

Shalom chaverim, shalom chaverim, shalom, shalom,
L'hit raut, l'hit raut, shalom, shalom,

Teach the children to sing the song smoothly and at a fairly slow pace but without dragging. When they can perform it fairly confidently, ask them to perform the following rhythmic pattern and to repeat it several times:

1	2	3	4
da	da	da - a	
♩	♩	♩	

When they can do this, ask one of the children to play the rhythm to the notes EGB as follows:

1	2	3	4
da	da	da - a	
♩	♩	♩	
E	G	B	

Now add this to the tune as the rest of the class sing it.

When they can do this, divide the singers into three groups. Each group should enter when the previous one has reached the point marked with an asterisk. The accompaniment will have to be extended at the end and the performer should play the pattern until all the singers have finished singing. Then, to give a sense of completion, it should be performed once more.

Purpose

To introduce the children to the concepts of major and minor keys and to enable them to identify whether a tune is in a major key or in a minor key; to teach them a new song in a minor key which can be sung as a three-part canon with an ostinato accompaniment.

Resources

Cassette: side 4, activity 77
Copymaster 86
Chime bars: EGB

Presentation:

Ask the children to listen to the tune of 'Happy Birthday' on the cassette and to sing it along with the music. When they have done this, play them the second version and ask them to sing that as well. Now involve them in a discussion of the two versions. Draw their attention to the fact that the second version sounds far sadder than the first.

Explain to them that the first version – the 'happier'

78. IS IT MAJOR OR IS IT MINOR?

Purpose
To give the children practice in determining whether a musical extract is in a major key or a minor key.

Resources
Cassette: side 4, activity 78
Copymaster 87

Presentation:
Remind the children about the work done on major and minor scales in Activity 77. Explain to them that they are now going to hear several musical extracts which are either in a major or a minor scale. They must listen very carefully and decide which extract is in which type of scale and then enter the answers on the copymaster.

The correct answers are as shown here:

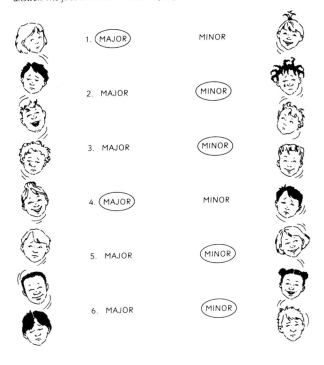

LISTENING PUZZLE 9

IS IT MAJOR OR IS IT MINOR?

You will hear six tunes played on the tape. Listen to each one very carefully and decide whether it is major or minor. Draw a circle round your answer. The first two have been done for you.

1. (MAJOR)   MINOR

2. MAJOR   (MINOR)

3. MAJOR   (MINOR)

4. (MAJOR)   MINOR

5. MAJOR   (MINOR)

6. MAJOR   (MINOR)

79. COMPOSING A MINOR MELODY

Purpose
To extend the children's understanding of major and minor tonalities further by giving them the opportunity to compose their own melodies in a minor key.

Resources
Copymaster 88
Chime bars: C D E♭(=D#) F G A♭ (=G#) B C'

Presentation:
Start by helping the children to clap out the rhythmic pattern on the copymaster. They will probably find it easiest if they identify the syllables for each note and then clap them out.

When they have mastered this, ask them to experiment with the chime bars and produce a melody which starts on the low C and finishes on the high C. The other suggestions are put there to help the children

given a coherent shape to their melodies. It is important to remember that they are no more than suggestions and there is no need to bind a child to them if that child can produce a melody which 'sounds right' but which uses different melodic ideas. In all composition work, it is the sound which decides whether the work is satisfactory, not arid theory.

As in earlier activities of this type, encourage the children to try out their ideas, to play them to each other for criticism and then to experiment further in order to refine their ideas and decide on a final version. When that has been achieved, ask them to write out the names of the notes on the copymaster. These scores can then be used to enable the composer or other people to reproduce the melody. Remember that the children should experiment with the sound first. Do not allow them simply to write the names of notes down at random and then to play them. Notation is simply there to capture what has already been played and heard.

80. MUSIC FROM INDIA

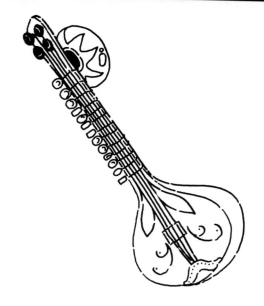

Purpose
To introduce the children to the sound of Indian music; to give them a very basic understanding of how the music is constructed; to enable them to improvise their own music on a particular scale (or *thāt* as it is known in Indian music).

Resources
Cassette: side 4, activity 80
Copymaster 89

Presentation:
Play the children the music on the cassette. Do this several times and ask the children to listen particularly to the instruments which are being played. Explain to them that the string sounds are played on a sitār and the drum sounds on a tablā. Draw their attention to the pictures of these instruments on the copymaster.

Explain to them that in Indian music a melody is called a *ragā* (pronounced rahg). Remind them that they have been playing music based on particular orders of notes known as scales. Sometimes these scales are said to be major and sometimes minor. These are not the only types of scale possible: in fact there are probably as many different types of scales in the world as there are languages. In Indian music, the term for a scale is *thāt* and each scale has its own name. The piece which they have just heard is called 'rāg Desh' and is based on a scale called 'Khāmajo'.

Extension
Using the Indian scale on the copymaster, ask the children to make up their own raga.

81. MARCH OF THE WOMEN

Purpose
To introduce the children to the music of Ethel Smyth and to enable them to begin to put it into a historical and social context.

Resources
Cassette: side 4, activity 81
Copymaster 90

Background information
For hundreds of years, only the wealthiest people in this country were allowed to vote and to decide on how the country was going to be governed. Even when, in the 19th century, others were given the vote, it was only men who received it. Women were not regarded as being important enough to vote, however wealthy they were. Many of them, of course, saw this as an insult and began to protest. In 1903, Mrs Emily Pankhurst founded the Women's Social and Political Union. This group began to write to politicians, to hold meetings and to publish pamphlets demanding the vote for women. Since the word for the right to vote is 'suffrage', they became known as the 'Suffragettes'. One of the songs which became very popular amongst the Suffragettes, who sang it on marches, at meetings and during riots, was 'The March of the Women' by Ethel Smyth. Smyth was a successful composer who gave up her career for a while in order to dedicate herself entirely to helping the women's cause. In 1912, she was found guilty of

99

smashing the windows of a cabinet minister's house and was sentenced to two months in Holloway Prison.

While she was there, she was visited by a very famous conductor of the day, Sir Thomas Beecham. Afterwards he told of his amusement and surprise to find, when he arrived, a group of women singing the March of the Women at the tops of their voices in the exercise yard below, while the composer Ethel Smyth conducted them with a toothbrush through the bars of her cell window.

Presentation:
Listen to the recording of the 'March of the Women', encouraging the children to imagine what the meetings of the suffragettes would have been like. You could draw on material from history text books to help you at this point.

Background information
Ethel Smyth was born in 1858, the daughter of a major general in the British army. In those days, women were very much discouraged from pursuing a career, including in music. Those women who did become professional musicians tended to become performers. To become a composer was a very rare thing indeed and it was virtually unheard of for young women students to study composition.

Ethel Smyth fought against all these restrictions. When she told her father that she wanted to become a composer, he told her that he would rather see her dead. But, ignoring this, she went to Leipzig in Germany to study with some of the foremost composition teachers of the day. She had several works performed in Germany before returning to England where she produced her Mass in D, said by leading critics of the day to equal the

works of Beethoven. From there she progressed to writing operas and made history by becoming the first woman ever to have an opera performed at the world famous Metropolitan Opera House in New York.

Presentation
Using the cassette, **Copymaster 90** and the advice included in the introduction to the book, teach the children to perform 'The March of the Women'. Encourage them to produce a full, confident sound, with a good volume but without shouting.

Starting note: C
Count in: 1 2 3 4 1 2 3 4

March of the Women

Shout, shout, up with your song!
Cry with the wind, for the dawn is breaking;
March, march, swing you along,
Wide blows our banner, and hope is waking.
Song with its story, dreams with their glory,
Lo! they call, and glad is their word!
Forward! Hark how it swells
Thunder of freedom, the voice of the Lord!

Life, strife – these two are one,
Naught can ye win but by faith and daring.
On, on – that ye have done
But for the work of today preparing.
Firm in reliance, laugh a defiance,
(Laugh in hope, for sure is the end)
March, march – many as one,
Shoulder to shoulder and friend to friend.

82. COMPOSE A MARCH

da   di-di   da   di-di

A second instrument could then play on the first beat each time.

● The unpitched instruments could play a combination of the above.
● A further possibility is for the children to keep the beat by playing a two-note ostinato (see glossary) on a pitched instrument at a pitch lower than the melody. Precisely which notes they use will, of course, depend on the notes used for the melody (see below) and this element might best be introduced at a later point, when the melody has been finalised.

From here you can move to focusing on the pitched instruments. These could be arranged in a variety of ways. You could simply give the children a xylophone or metallophone with the notes arranged in the conventional sequence. Alternatively, you could give each group a variety of arrangements of notes on which to improvise.

● Group 1 could be given the following chime bars: C D E F G A B C', i.e. the scale of C major.
● Group 2 could be asked to improvise on an F major scale, i.e. notes: F G A Bb C' D' E' F'.
● Group 3 could work on a minor scale, e.g. C D Eb (=D#) F G Ab (=G#) B C'.
● Group 4 could use a pentatonic scale such as those formed by all the black notes on the chime bars or the keyboard, i.e. C# D# (=Eb) F# G#(=Ab) Bb (=A#).
● For the fifth group, you could simply mix up the notes on xylophone or metallophone at random. This often produces the best results in a project of this type because the sounds are less predictable and more exciting.

Precisely which arrangement you choose to use will obviously depend on the instrumental resources available to you. You might choose to return to this activity from time to time and adopt a different set of notes as a basis for the melodic aspect of the work.

Once the children have been given a specific set of pitches, they should work on producing their melodies along the same lines as those already outlined on pages 13–16 and at other points in this book, i.e. through experimentation, presentation, group and self criticism, further experimentation, synthesis of ideas and final performance of the melody. This can then be superimposed onto the accompaniment; a process which will inevitably lead to further adaptations and development of ideas.

When the final performance stage has been reached, give the children the opportunity to perform live to their peers and other groups in the school and the community and to record their music on cassette.

Purpose

To extend children's composition experiences by giving them the opportunity to produce their own marching music; to enable them to use a variety of scales for this purpose.

Resources

Several sets of instruments, each of which should include four or five instruments, pitched and unpitched. Space for movement

Presentation:

Tap out a steady beat on a tambour and ask the children to march round the room in time to this. This way they will feel the clear pattern of 1 2 1 2 to their movements. This should be felt as an underlying basis for the marches that they are now going to produce.

The next step is to divide the children into groups. Draw their attention to the fact that the particular group of instruments to which they have been assigned include pitched and unpitched percussion instruments. Suggest to them that the unpitched percussion could be used to maintain the beat. However, it would be very boring if the beat were simply maintained by one instrument playing throughout. Therefore they might start by experimenting with ways of maintaining the beat, while at the same time maintaining musical interest. The following are just some of the ways in which they might do this. No doubt your class will be able to extend the possibilities in many ways.

● Two unpitched instruments could be used, with one playing on every beat and the other playing on the second beat each time.
● One unpitched instrument could play a very basic rhythm such as:

83. IMPROVISATION ON AFRICAN SCALES ▶

Purpose
To extend the children's appreciation of the fact that world music makes use of a variety of scales by giving them the opportunity to improvise on African scales.

Resources
3 sets of pitched instruments with the following sets of notes:
  Set 1: C E F# G B C'
  Set 2: C E*b* F G A B C'
  Set 3: C E*b* F# A C'

Presentation
Remind the children of the work already done on major and minor scales and on ragas. Explain to them that, in the countries of Africa, there are large numbers of scales in use. The children are now going to be given the opportunity to improvise their own melodies based on

three such scales. They will notice that each scale has a different number of notes within it: the first has six, the second seven and the third has five notes. This shows that the numbers of notes, like the order of pitches, can vary considerably, a fact that is not always made clear to children when their experience focuses entirely on eighteenth and nineteenth century western European music.

From here, the process of improvisation will follow the cycle of experimentation, presentation, criticism, further experimentation, refinement and settling on a final version, on which a great deal of the work in this book is based and which has been outlined in detail on pages 13–16.

When the children have completed their melodies, play them some examples of African music. They might then wish to return to their compositions and refine them further in the light of what they have heard.

84. GO DOWN MOSES ▶

Purpose
To introduce the children to spirituals through performance and listening; to enable them to begin to understand the social and historical origins of such songs; to give them further experience of singing a song in a minor key; of singing a verse and chorus song and of adding a simple pitched percussion accompaniment to it; to give them further experience of identifying the characteristics of a song which reflect the mood of the words.

Resources
Cassette: side 4, activity 84
Chime bars: G, A, B, C

Bass metallophone/xylophone: E B C (If this instrument is not available use further chime bars or the piano. In the case of the piano, you will need the piano chart from Copymasters 37 and 38)
Copymaster 91

Presentation
Explain to the children that, thousands of years ago, the Israelites living in Egypt were forced to become slaves and to perform back-breaking tasks in the most inhuman conditions. Eventually one of their number, a man called Moses, led an uprising against the pharaoh or king of the Egyptians and led the Israelites across the Red Sea and the Sinai desert into the land of Israel. The song below describes the feelings of the Israelites during their oppression.

Now teach the children the words and tune of the following song.

Starting note: B,
Count in: 1 2 3 4 1 2 3 (NB The first word starts on the fourth and last beat of the bar).

Go Down Moses

Verse	When Israel was in Egypt's land
Chorus	Let my people go!
Verse	Oppressed so hard they could not stand
Chorus	Let my people go!
	Go down Moses
	Way down in Egypt's land
Verse	Tell old Pharaoh
Chorus	Let my people go!

When Is-rael was in E-gypt's land Let my peo-ple go! Op-

pressed so hard they could not stand Let my peo-ple go

Go down___ Mo-ses___ Way down in E-gypt's___ land___

Tell old___ Pha-rao Let my peo-ple go.

When the children can sing the tune and the words fairly confidently, add the instrumental accompaniment from **Copymaster 91**. For this, you will need two players, one on the chime bars and one on the metallophone/xylophone/piano. Practise playing the accompaniment to the rhythm:

1	2	3	4
da	- a	da	- a

Draw the children's attention to the fact that the song is in a verse and chorus form. Accentuate this by arranging for a soloist or small group to sing the tune, with a larger group of singers performing the chorus.

When they have performed the song a few times, ask the children to tell you whether the music is in a major or minor key. (It sounds very sad and therefore is in a minor key.) Explain to them that this key accentuates the mood of the music and conveys the oppression experienced by the Israelites.

From here, you can go on to explain to the children that this song was actually first sung by a group of people who themselves were experiencing very similar circumstances to the Israelites. These were the people whose families had been captured in Africa and transported in terrible conditions to America where they worked in slavery. These people compared themselves to the Israelites and sang songs expressing a yearning for freedom. Very often the songs draw on images from the Bible.

103

GLOSSARY OF MUSICAL TERMS

Accent
Imitate the sound of a clock ticking. Say 'tick, tock, tick, tock' regularly. Now repeat the exercise and clap every time you say 'tick'. The 'tick' now sounds louder than the sounds next to it. Therefore it is said to be an accented sound. In music, an accented note is one which is louder and given greater emphasis than others.

Accompaniment
The accompaniment is the 'backing' to a performer or group of performers. If you sing a folk song and someone plays the guitar along with you, the guitar is said to be providing the accompaniment. It is possible to be accompanied by others or to accompany yourself. It is also possible for the accompaniment to be provided by a large number of instruments. In an opera, for example, the accompaniment is often provided by a full orchestra.

Arranging
Arranging is the process of taking an existing piece of music and developing it in some way. For example, a well known pop song might have its words removed and be arranged so that it is played by instruments only. Another example might be to add an accompaniment to a solo tune.

Beat (or pulse)
When you listen to a piece of music, you often find yourself tapping your feet or moving your head regularly with it, rather as if you were a clock. When you do this, you are reacting to the underlying beat or pulse of the music. When soldiers march to music, they move in time to the beat. Not all music has a regular beat or pulse. If you listen to church music from the Medieval period, for example, you will not find it very easy to feel a steady beat.

Composing
This is the act of thinking up musical ideas, putting them together and building them up into an original piece of music.

Dynamics
This is the term used to refer to the loudness or softness of sounds. Therefore, when a conductor tells a group of performers to 'notice the dynamics', he or she is asking them to make sure that they are paying attention to the differences in volume indicated by the composer.

Dynamics are traditionally indicated by a series of signs, e.g.

ff: very loud
f: loud
mf: moderately loud
mp: moderately soft
p: soft
pp: very soft.

Elements
These are the building blocks of music such as pitch, duration, pace, timbre, texture, dynamics, and structure.

Glissando
If you take a beater and slide it from left to right or right to left on a xylophone or glockenspiel, it produces a rapid sequence of notes. This is known as a 'glissando'. You can produce a glissando on the piano by sliding the back of your fingers rapidly up or down the keys.

Harmony
Harmony is produced when two or more sounds are performed at the same time.

High or low notes
You will find high notes on the right hand side of the piano; low ones on the left. In staff notation, the higher the pitch of a note, the higher it is placed on the stave. The lower its pitch, the lower its position will be. In this way, the stave acts as a kind of graph to show the rise and fall of the musical pitches.

Improvise
This is the word applied to the process of making up the music as you are performing. Jazz musicians make a great use of improvisation.

Melody
A melody is a series of sounds which move upwards or downwards or are repeated to produce a tune.

Ostinato
If you play a series of notes over and over again as an accompaniment to a melody, this is known as playing an 'ostinato'.

Pace
This refers to the speed at which the underlying beat of a piece of music goes and is also referred to by the Italian word, *tempo.*

Phrase
Listen to a singer performing. The singer does not keep singing a series of notes which go on indefinitely. Every now and again, he or she will take a quick breath or sing a slightly longer note or come to a short stop. This breaks up the music in much the same way that we break up speech so that we do not sound like Daleks. These sections into which music is divided are known as phrases. It is not only singers who produce phrases in

music. You will also notice the same effect if you listen to instrumentalists performing.

Pitch

We use the term pitch when we are referring to whether notes are high or low notes.

Pitched (or tuned) percussion

These are percussion instruments which have notes of different pitches and on which it is therefore possible to play tunes. Please see the introductory section to the book where you will find details of the types of pitched percussion instruments commonly available.

Pulse

See *Beat*.

Repetition

When two or more notes in a row are at the same pitch, they are said to be repeated. A collection of notes, or a particular rhythmic pattern, can be repeated as can a whole section of music.

Rhythm

This refers to the way that long notes, short notes and silences are combined in music.

Rhythmic pattern

A group of long and short sounds.

Scale

A scale is a basic group of notes from which a melody or longer piece of music can be built. There are probably as many different types of scales as there are languages and dialects in the world. Many of the tunes in this book are built on what is known as a major scale. To play an example of a major scale arrange your chime bars as follows:

C D E F G A B C

(Each bar should be slightly smaller than the one to its left. The letter names of the notes are stamped on the bars themselves.) If you now play each note in sequence from left to right you will be playing what is known as a C major scale. If you want to play the same scale on the piano, this is what you do:

i. Look at the black notes. You will notice these are arranged in alternating groups of two and three notes.

ii. Choose one group of two black notes.

iii. Look for the white note immediately to the left of the lower of the two black notes.

iv. Starting with that note and moving from left to right play the eight white notes next to each other in order.

Signs

The length or pitch of a note can be shown through a number of visual indications. A high note, for example, could be indicated by holding the arms high in the air and a low note by crouching down. In the same way, a group of three short notes and a long note could be shown by arranging a series of objects, such as building blocks as follows: ☐ ☐ ☐ ▭

Structure

This refers to the way that a piece of music has been put together so that some sections are the same as, or contrast with, others.

Style

Dress designers use particular patterns to produce garments which are individual to them. From one historical period to another and from one country to another, styles of dress change. The same is true of music. The way in which a composer puts together the elements of music results in a particular style. This can vary from one composer to another, from one generation to another and from one country to another.

Symbols

These are the written signs used to show which notes are to be performed, at what pitch, for how long, how loudly or quietly, on their own or with other notes, how quickly or slowly. There are many different types of symbols used in music, e.g. staff notation, graphic notation, solfa, chord indications, etc.

Texture

Texture refers to the way that sounds and melodies are combined and blended together in music. Sometimes, the texture will be such that a particular melody is heard as being more important than any of the other sounds being performed. At other times, there might be several instruments playing together, every one of which seems to have an equally important tune to play. This is very similar to the situation in textiles where sometimes one colour or a particular type of fabric is made to stand out from the others. At other times, all the elements are equally important and the material is smooth and closely woven.

Tempo (plural: Tempi)

This is the term used for the speed at which a piece of music is played.

Timbre

Imagine a note of the same pitch and length being sung by a man, a woman, or a child, and being played on the violin, the trumpet and the piano. The note would not change in pitch or length but its quality would change so that you would hardly be likely to think that the male voice was the sound of a trumpet. This distinctive quality of a sound is known as its 'timbre'. The term 'tone colour' is also sometimes used to describe it.

Unison

Sing 'Three Blind Mice'. Now sing it along with someone else. When two or more people perform the same tune at the same time and in the same way, they are said to be performing in unison. This is different from 'harmony' where two or more people perform together but perform different notes from each other.

Unpitched (or untuned) percussion

These are percussion instruments on which it is not possible to play tunes.